THE REVELATION OF
AMERICA
IN
PROPHECY

THE REVELATION OF
AMERICA
IN
PROPHECY

THE GOSPEL
AMERICA'S POWER
THE WORLD'S HOPE

BY

SHERLOCK BALLY

LOGOS TO RHEMA PUBLISHING
8210 E. 71st STREET #250
TULSA, OK 74133

(918) 488-9667

COPYRIGHT PAGE

LOGOS TO RHEMA PUBLISHING
(918) 488-9667

THE REVELATION OF AMERICA IN PROPHECY

Copyright ©1997
Revised Edition ©2001
Logos To Rhema Publishing

ISBN 1 885591-71-3
Library of Congress Control Number: 2001094265

ALL RIGHTS RESERVED

Scripture quotations noted NIV are taken from the Holy Bible, New International Version® Copyright©1973,1978,1984, by International Bible Society. Used by permission of Zondervan Bible Publishing House. All rights reserved.

Printed in the USA by
Morris Publishing
3212 East Highway 30
Kearney, NE 68847
1-800-650-7888

Acknowledgments

It has been an interesting experience watching the hand of God put this book together through the gifts of special and dedicated people. It takes a lot to coordinate schedules and put together a finished product. Thanks to you all.

Dedication

This book is dedicated to my dear wife Reneé, whose support over the last twenty-six years has made it possible to fulfill the plan of God for my life.

To my two children, Rachel and Micah, whose love and care have been a great encouragement to me.

To my dear mother, whose unceasing intercession has kept me in crisis times.

Preface

The pronouncements of the demise of America are many. Reports of her irreversible decline are coming from all quarters and these reports seal her doom. As I examine scripture, I see that the principles and counsels of God are immutable. His love demands the protection of His people and His justice demands the judgment of sin.

God never judges or destroys before the people of God are warned and given the opportunity to leave. I understand the necessity for judgment on sin, yet minds have been so saturated with the evil around them that the very reason for the diversion of God's judgment has been overlooked!

The presence of the righteous would have saved Sodom and Gomorrah, and the judgment of God would have been averted.

My reason for writing this book came from the unavoidable doctrine that saturates my being on the presence, power and purposes for the people of God on this earth. I could not overlook the providence of God as he used America to release the greatest surge of evangelism in the history of the world. I could not overlook the remnant of praying, preaching and praising people who cannot be bought or compromised by the seductions of the world. I could no longer let the presence of sin blind men to the abounding grace of God.

God's revelation was like fire shut up in my bones and I could no longer be silent. The church is not anemic. America is not lost forever. God still has the destiny of this nation in His hands. As long as we call upon Him in complete surrender, this country will continue to be a beacon to the world.

This book emphasizes that point and commands the continuance of the church and the gospel in this crisis hour.

The church is alive, and it is the most powerful body of people on the face of the earth today!

TABLE OF CONTENTS

Chapter One

America's Prophetic Destiny

I believe the greatest injustice has been done to America when it comes to relating where she fits into Bible prophecy. This is one of the major reasons for the writing of this book. I hope it will so stir your spirit that you will never see America again apart from her God. There are three streams of prophetic revelation of end time fulfillment. These streams of prophetic revelation relate to the Jew, Gentile and the Church of God. Built into prophecy, in relationship to the church of God, is a prophetic revelation with explosive power. A great oversight has taken place. The church, America's priceless treasure, has been overlooked! We must consider God's pivotal dealings with the church in order to understand God's dealings with the world.

If Satan can blind us to God's unparalleled purpose for the true church of Jesus Christ then he has blinded us to our identify, our destiny and our destination. Revelation 3:7 says, "And to the angel of the church in Philadelphia write; These things saith he that is holy, he that is true, he that hath the key of David, he that openeth and no man shutteth, and shutteth and no man openeth;"

Prophetically, we understand very clearly this is a reference to God's end time remnant or body of Christ. This is validated by verse ten, "Because thou hast kept the word of my patience, I also will keep thee from the hour of temptation, which shall come upon all the world, to try them that dwell upon the earth." The church is taken out from the hour of temptation which will try the entire earth. There is no trial that has ever tried the entire earth except the coming seven-year tribulation. This church has been taken out of that period. The promise of verse seven to this end time church is that God would sovereignly open a door no man can shut, and those people who walk through that door are walking into the end time harvest.

It is in this prophetic church position that America has two of the greatest assignments ever given a nation. Yes, it is the land of the free and home of the brave, but it is also the country that has been given an end time prophetic purpose of bringing in the largest harvest of souls for the kingdom of God and standing on the side of Israel as a prophetic covering. I Corinthians 10:32 says, "Give none offence, neither to the Jews, nor to the Gentiles, nor to the church of God:"

America you have believed the greatest lie ever perpetuated on the face of the earth. You have yielded yourself to the deceptive voice of the media and its atheistic and humanistic views. Its very purpose is to blind and numb you to your greatness that, without a shout against the tyranny, you will lay down your divine prophetic purpose because the Saturday night news convinces you all is lost.

I believe the church is the legitimate end time spiritual superpower of the world. Christian leaders and their flocks have missed America's prophetic place. It is not found in its arsenal of super weapons, its economy or even in its political system. The true church is the greatest force upon the face of the earth and America is the greatest repository for that source of power.

America look at the roots and the tree from which you sprang and you will see God has planned and purposed it to be so. I think one of the greatest gifts to all mankind was the divine plan and purpose of God to establish America for her prophetic assignment. America is the most prominent exponent of the Christian faith the world has ever seen, and therein lies her power.

America look back from whence you came. In 1831, Lyman Beecher wrote in the newspaper entitled, *The Spirit of the Pilgrims:* "The government of God is the only government which will hold society, against depravity within and temptation without; and this it must do by the force of its own law written upon the heart. This is that unity of the Spirit and that bond of peace which can alone perpetuate national purity and tranquillity, that law of universal and impartial love by which alone nations can be kept back from ruin. There is no safety for republics but in self-government, under the influence of a holy heart, swayed by the government of God." 1.

America, that government of God, the only government that will hold society, is still yours and it has not lost one ounce of its power. That government was the basis for the formation of America — it is the gospel of Jesus Christ! The evangelistic heart of the early forefathers brought them to this land to create a nation for the purpose, plan and glory of God. That has not changed!

If we let Satan's power to deceive, darken, destroy and bludgeon the true church of Jesus Christ into submission to a compromised lifestyle or destruction we give up our prophetic position and purpose. That will not happen to the true church because we have been set in prophetic order for such a time as this. Church we are about to have our finest hour!

It is important to tell you a little about my background then you will understand why I must be a voice calling out in this dark hour of deception over America. My name is Sherlock Bally and I was saved at the age of seventeen. I was born of East Indian parents on the island of Trinidad, in the Caribbean. I was a rebellious child and by the age of sixteen, the ravages of sin ripped my heart, mind and soul apart. I sowed the seeds of rebellion and resentment—my indulgence in an immoral life had come to the point of full reaping. My mind was completely inclined to sin and my body obeyed the commands so easily given it. With disregard for all formal and parental authority I was master of my own fate.

Soon, however, I discovered I was trapped by vice and habits, and totally absorbed in the sins of the world. My school professors questioned me as to why I was not applying myself and failing courses when my abilities far exceeded my grades. My school days were only an avenue for more pleasure as I was surrounded by many whose only motive in life was pleasure.

The details of my indulgences are unnecessary to explain, but the results in my life were devastating. The realm of sin and pleasure left me, at sixteen, in a spirit of extreme hopelessness. This void permeated every area of my life. I rarely spoke because of a severe stammering problem; and I had a growth in my nasal passage, which caused me great sickness.

It was at this point, when everything in my life was going in the wrong direction and taking me to an early grave, that I was invited to attend a full gospel service being held by American missionaries. I must admit my motives for attending the service were less than honorable. Little did I know that night that was about to change the whole course of my life.

After the preaching I walked to the altar, which I realize, in itself, was an absolute miracle. I realized a great truth that night — all I needed to set me free was Jesus! That was a revelation I knew came only from God. After my prayer of surrender to Jesus extraordinary things happened. My mind was healed, my physical conditions were healed, my heart was totally and completely transformed, my stammering was instantly lifted and God called me into the ministry. The words of God have never left me, "From your mother's womb I have chosen you. I long to use you. I will give you many souls." I left that place knowing in my heart I had met the true and living God. His name is Jesus.

Soon after that wonderful experience of salvation, I was sent to Southern Bible College in Houston, Texas. I then returned to Trinidad and became the pastor of the very church I was saved in. God never ceases to amaze me! While in college I met my wife Reneé Taber. We were married in 1975 and this young lady, who had never left the shores of America, accompanied me on a journey back to the island of Trinidad. For the next fifteen years we worked together and watched God do a mighty work in the island.

The church grew wonderfully and soon we had our own prophetic, nationally viewed television program. We also had a radio ministry that was heard over a wide area. From this exposure I found myself being asked to speak at conventions, seminars, crusades and revivals throughout the Caribbean. Everything seemed right in my little world.

It was at this time of great growth and national recognition, with the doors swinging open throughout the Caribbean, that God began to deal with me to go to America as a missionary! It sounded so ridiculous that I tried to put it from my thoughts. My first response was it could not be God; it must only be the excessive exercise of my imagination. Was I Lot, blessed with the green pastures of Jordan, but still looking for the better life? No, I was here in the Caribbean with great response to the call of God on my life. The prophecy and end-time ministry of the television station was so popular God could not possibly be saying give it all up and go to Oklahoma!

I was pastoring, we had a school teaching on the book of Revelation, and I had a wonderful group of local people working with me in the church. God would not move me to Oklahoma. It was humorous to me, but I couldn't shake the nudging and prompting of the Holy Spirit. Nevertheless, I decided to stay in Trinidad. There, that's it. God could get someone else. I had too much to do.

Then on July 27, 1990, the impossible happened. I was at the National Television studios to do my television program with my team. That night there was an attempted coup, an effort to overthrow the democratic government of Trinidad. The Parliament was held hostage and the television studio came under direct attack. The studio was shot up and commandeered by a fundamentalist Islamic group. I was in the studio preaching at that moment on "The Spirit of Antichrist and Lawlessness." (Nothing like an illustrated sermon). I heard hundreds of rounds of ammunition outside the studio. All we could do was pray and wait. We did both.

Those minutes seemed like hours. The programming was halted and here they came men with fire in their eyes, with knives, pistols, shotguns and AK 47's. The nightmare was real. I should have listened and gone to America was the thought that crossed my mind. Here we were captured and not knowing if we would be alive tomorrow. We were held hostage by a group of inflamed men who believed their assignment came from God. Now they were here in the studio along with commentators, news personnel and others. We would not be released until the government met the demands of our captors.

The country went into a panic. Fires, lootings, shootings and all that comes with rebellion filled the great little island called, "Land of the Hummingbird." I understood that something would have to be done in the supernatural realm if we were going to live. During the first few hours of our crisis, prayer was offered by my team of seven and myself. Providentially, this was the first program my wife Reneé had missed. Reneé was the coproducer of the program, but could not make the filming that night. Immediately, I realized the grace of God as Reneé's production booth was the one area of the studio totally destroyed by gunfire. I thank God that I did not have the extra burden of worry for the lives of my wife and children.

Our captors made it perfectly clear we would be there until the whole situation was resolved and the government capitulated and accepted their terms. Miraculously, just hours after our captivity the leader of the group pointed to me and my team and said words that still live within me, "You can go!" We did not debate or question. The others in the station were held for five additional days and were wired to be bombed twice!

The attempted coup was world news for three days. Many people were killed and much of our main city was burned. I will always be thankful for the release that day of my team and friends. God really does know how much you can endure and the next time I heard the Lord say, "Go to America," I didn't wait. I had learned a great lesson — *obedience is what God really wants out of us.* It is not our job to reason out the request and make sense of it, our duty and responsibility is to just obey.

Within a month of the attack my family and I were on an airplane heading for Tulsa, Oklahoma. When your life is in the hands of God, he knows how to direct and order providence to work on your behalf and even transform what the devil plans for evil into purposes that accelerate his divine plans for you.

America you must see the continuing providence and sovereignty of God over your land. If the power of the resurrected Christ could so deliver and save a miserable man like me and turn him into a preacher of the Gospel of Jesus Christ for the glory of God, then what great plan has God for the true church in America? You are not one soul filled with the living power of God, but millions! How foolish it must have sounded to the Reverend Gerald and Ellen Keele, missionaries of God, when the voice of God instructed them to go to Trinidad. Thank God they obeyed. I grew and was sent out from their labor of love and today they are among my most precious friends. I am a result of God's sovereignty and divine providence.

America you also are the result of God's sovereignty and divine providence. This country was founded out of the greatest missionary quest the world has ever known. The Puritans had faith and believed God was telling them to go. It sounded strange to them also, but they went enduring hardness and death, and established, by their great faith in Jesus Christ, the most beautiful nation the world has ever seen, the city on a hill, America is the beacon to the world.

Church we are at our finest hour in history and God is still a God of principle. If Sodom and Gomorrah would have been spared for ten righteous then I believe God has not changed his mind concerning this predestined, predetermined, miraculous nation and her role in fulfilling Bible prophecy. If the power of Christ can transform one life so completely think what can be done in a nation filled with the greatest source of that power on the face of the earth. America God shed his grace on thee.

Pastors, teachers, evangelists, apostles and prophets arise and shout the wake up call. The greatest harvest the world has ever seen is about to begin. America you are essential to this great hour! You are prepared for this great harvest now throw in the sickle and reap the wheat you have sown (in my life and millions like me) around the world. The church is alive and moving in the resurrection power of Almighty God.

America your job is not over. The gospel found between your shores is the only hope that exists for the world today! There is enough power in your midst to do what seems impossible.

Church of America come forth! I command you in the name of the Lord to come forth!

Chapter Two

One Nation Under God

One cannot go back and trace the history of America without coming to this conclusion America was founded with a divine destiny planted in the hearts of the forefathers. This country was established upon Christian beliefs and most of the legal documents of this great nation directly implore the will of God Almighty to preserve and keep this nation. The constitutions of all fifty states in America without exception has an appeal to prayer or includes a prayer to Almighty God of the universe. It is very clear from our forefathers that God was at the head of every decision. His wisdom was needed to guide and rule this great nation established from Christian principles. Let's take a look at a brief summary of thoughts, opinions, prayers and acts from some of the greatest leaders of this great nation.

George Washington prayed, "And now, Almighty Father, if it is Thy holy will that we shall obtain a place and name among the nations of the earth, grant that we may be enabled to show our gratitude for Thy goodness by our endeavors to fear and obey Thee. Bless us with Thy wisdom in our counsels, success in battle, and let all our victories be tempered with humanity. Endow, also, our enemies with enlightened minds, that they become sensible of their injustice, and willing to restore our liberty and peace. Grant the petition of Thy servant, for the sake of Him whom Thou has called Thy beloved Son; nevertheless, not my will, but Thine be done." [1]

The Revelation of America

John Adams addressed the Continental Congress on July 1, 1776. He spoke to the delegates from the Thirteen Colonies stating, "Before God, I believe the hour has come. My judgment approves this measure, and my whole heart is in it. All that I have, and all that I am, and all that I hope in this life, I am now ready here to stake upon it. And I leave off as I began, that live or die, survive or perish; I am for the Declaration. It is my living sentiment, and by the blessing of God it shall be my dying sentiment. Independence now, and Independence for ever!" 2.

John Quincy Adams, the sixth President of the United States, said: "I speak as a man of the world to men of the world; and I say to you, Search the Scriptures! The Bible is the book of all others, to be read at all ages, and in all conditions of human life; not to be read once or twice or thrice through, and then laid aside, but to be read in small portions of one or two chapters every day, and never to be intermitted, unless by some overruling necessity." 3.

Calvin Coolidge, the thirtieth President of the United States, had this to say about the Puritan forefathers of this country: "They were intent upon establishing a Christian commonwealth in accordance with the principle of self-government. They were an inspired body of men. It has been said that God sifted the nations that He might send choice grain into the wilderness....Who can fail to see in it the hand of destiny? Who can doubt that it has been guided by a Divine Providence?" 4.

The first Continental Congress was opened by prayer and the 35th Psalm was read: "Plead my cause, Oh, Lord, with them that strive with me, fight against them that fight against me. Take hold of buckler and shield, and rise up for my help. Draw also the spear and the battle-axe to meet those who pursue me; Say to my soul, 'I am your salvation.' Let those be ashamed and dishonored who seek my life; Let those be turned back and humiliated who devise evil against me...". 5.

It is very clear that the first Congress instituted prayer over this nation's law-making houses. Even the Supreme Court supported the concept of America formed under God for a divine purpose. Justice David Josiah Brewer gave this opinion in 1892: "Our laws and our institutions must necessarily be based upon and embody the teachings of the Redeemer of mankind. It is impossible that it should be otherwise; and in this sense and to this extent our civilization and our institutions are emphatically Christian.

"No purpose of action against religion can be imputed to any legislation, state or national, because this is a religious people. This is historically true. From the discovery of this continent to the present hour, there is a single voice making this affirmation.

"The commission to Christopher Columbus... [recited] that it is hoped that by God's assistance some of the continents and islands in the ocean will be discovered...

"The first colonial grant made to Sir Walter Raleigh in 1584.... and the grant authorizing him to enact statutes for the government of the proposed colony provided that they be not against the true Christian faith...

"The first charter of Virginia, granted by King James I in 1606....commenced the grant in these words: ...in propagating of Christian Religion to such People as yet live in Darkness...

"Language of similar import may be found in the subsequent charters of that colony.... in 1609 and 1611, and the same is true of the various charters granted to the other colonies. In language more or less emphatic is the establishment of the Christian religion declared to be one of the purposes of the grant. The celebrated compact made by the Pilgrims in the Mayflower, 1620 recites: Having undertaken for the Glory of God, and advancement of the Christian faith.... a voyage to plant the first colony in the northern parts of Virginia...

"The fundamental orders of Connecticut, under which a provisional government was instituted in 1638-1639, commence with this declaration: .... And well knowing where a people are gathered together the word of God requires that to maintain the peace and union....there should be an orderly and decent government established according to God....to maintain and preserve the liberty and purity of the gospel of our Lord Jesus which we now profess....of the said gospel [which] is now practised amongst us.'

"In the charter of privileges granted by William Penn to the province of Pennsylvania, in 1701, it is recited: ...no people can be truly happy, though under the greatest enjoyment of civil liberties, if abridged of....their religious profession and worship...

"Coming nearer to the present time, the Declaration of Independence recognizes the presence of the Divine in human affairs in these words: We hold these truths to be self-evident, that all men are created equal, that they are endowed by their Creator with certain unalienable Rights.... appealing to the Supreme Judge of the world for the rectitude of our intentions.... And for the support of this Declaration, with firm reliance on the Protection of

Divine Providence, we mutually pledge to each other our Lives, our Fortunes, and our sacred Honor.

"...We find everywhere a clear recognition of the same truth....because of a general recognition of this truth [that we are a Christian nation], the question has seldom been presented to the courts...

"There is no dissonance in these declarations. There is a universal language pervading them all, having one meaning; they affirm and reaffirm that this is a religious nation. These are not individual sayings, declarations of private persons: they are organic utterances; they speak the voice of the entire people.

"While because of a general recognition of this truth the question has seldom been presented to the courts, yet we find that in *Updegraph v. The Commonwealth*, it was decided that: Christianity, general Christianity, is, and always has been, a part of the common law....not Christianity with an established church....but Christianity with liberty of conscience to all men.

"And in *The People v. Ruggles,* Chancellor Kent, the great commentator on American law, speaking as Chief Justice of the Supreme Court of New York, said: The people of this State, in common with the people of this country, profess the general doctrines of Christianity, as the rule of their faith and practice....We are a Christian people, and the morality of the country is deeply engrafted upon Christianity, and not upon the doctrines or worship of those impostors [other religions].

"And in the famous case of *Vidal v. Girard's Executors* this Court...observed: It is also said, and truly, that the Christian religion is a part of the common law...

"If we pass beyond these matters to a view of American life as expressed by its laws, its business, its customs and its society, we find everywhere a clear recognition of the same truth. Among other matters note the following: The form of oath universally prevailing, concluding with an appeal to the Almighty; the custom of opening sessions of all deliberative bodies and most conventions with prayer; the prefatory words of all wills, "In the name of God, amen"; the laws respecting the observance of the Sabbath, with the general cessation of all secular business, and the closing of courts, legislatures, and other similar public assemblies on that day; the churches and church organizations which abound in every city, town and hamlet; the multitude of charitable organizations existing everywhere under Christian auspices; the gigantic missionary associations, with general support, and aiming to establish Christian missions in every quarter of the globe.

"These and many other matters which might be noticed, add a volume of unofficial declarations to the mass of organic utterances that this is a Christian nation....we find everywhere a clear recognition of the same truth." 6.

President Lincoln on March 30, 1863, issued a historic *Proclamation Appointing a National Fast Day:* "Whereas, the Senate of the United States devoutly recognizing the Supreme Authority and just Government of Almighty God in all the affairs of men and of nations, has, by a resolution, requested the President to designate and set apart a day for national prayer and humiliation: "And whereas, it is the duty of nations as well as of men to own their dependence upon the overruling power of God, to confess their sins and transgressions in humble sorrow yet with assured hope that genuine repentance will lead to mercy and pardon, and to recognize the sublime truth, announced in the Holy Scriptures and proven by all history: that those nations only are blessed whose God is the Lord...". 7.

President Theodore Roosevelt said, "Every thinking man, when he thinks, realizes that the teachings of the Bible are so interwoven and entwined with our whole civic and social life that it would be literally impossible for us to figure ourselves what that life would be if these standards were removed. We would lose almost all the standards by which we now judge both public and private morals; all the standards towards which we, with more or less resolution, strive to raise ourselves." 8.

Daniel Webster, one of the greatest speakers in America's history, said, "Lastly, our ancestors established their system of government on morality and religious sentiment. Moral habits, they believed, cannot safely be trusted on any other foundation than religious principle, nor any government be secure which is not supported by moral habits....Whatever makes men good Christians, makes them good citizens." 9.

On June 14, 1954, President Eisenhower gave his support to the Congressional Act, which added the phrase "under God," to the *Pledge of Allegiance*, by signing it into law, saying, "In this way we are reaffirming the transcendence of religious faith in America's heritage and future; in this way we shall constantly strengthen those spiritual weapons which forever will be our country's most powerful resource in peace and war." 10.

18.   The Revelation of America

It is more than apparent when you look at the history of America that its greatness is found in the gospel of Jesus Christ. America this is still your greatest asset.

Chapter Three

The Nations And Prophecy

There are three sets of people that have deep involvement in end-time Bible prophecy: The Jews, the Gentiles (nations) and the Church (body of Christ). There are specific prophecies that relate to the Gentiles of the nations of the world and these prophecies give a detailed scenario of the future of the nations and they give clear definition to the present trends that are being seen among the nations. The political, military and economic conditions are given full treatment in the scripture, so by having a clear understanding of the prophecies that relate to these nations, we see the conditions and events leading to an appointment with prophetic destiny.

What a joy it brings to this hour to see the superintending hand of God in the affairs of men to such an extent that we know that God has never, and will never, abdicate His throne and that all these conditions and occurrences are leading to the final consummation of all things. He still has the whole wide world in His hands!

The one thing that defines and pervades all that is happening is that all these conditions in the nations are heading to one prophetic climax, the coming of the King of Kings and the Lord of Lords. There is no renegade nation that operates apart from the sovereignty of God, no philosophy, ideal, politic, or religion that stakes a claim to independent action apart from the fulfilling of the ultimate will of God. The destinies of these nations are seen in scripture with great clarity, with no room left for private negotiation. Their choice is simple, follow God and His Word or pay the price for rejection and rebellion.

Many people in leadership have pronounced their curses of doom upon this great land of America. They have said it is spiritless, anemic, irrelevant and woefully powerless. This great mistake is made by concentrating on the negative. By concentrating on the visible conditions in the political, economical, military and apostate religious realm, we exhibit a disregard for the supernatural power of the real body of Christ. Yes, there are problems, but there is also a great Redeemer who can change lives in an instant. When we constantly focus on the problems we begin to think they are more powerful than the true resource of power each believer retains. All the antichrist system can do is deceive the souls of men and cause them to forget who they are in Christ. God predestined and predetermined that America would be the country from which His care and love, as seen in the spread of the gospel, would flow to the rest of the world. He preordained that the true church of Jesus Christ would love and protect Israel.

Matthew 24:3-4, "And as he sat upon the mount of Olives, the disciples came unto him privately, saying, Tell us, when shall these things be? And what shall be the sign of thy coming, and of the end of the world? And Jesus answered and said unto them, Take heed that no man deceive you."

In response to the question of the disciples concerning the sign of Jesus' coming, His answer was amazing, "Take heed that no man deceive you. "Deception would be the qualifying sign of the end of time and the motives and purposes of the devil, the antichrist, and the false prophet, this trinity of evil, would be pervasively deceptive. As dangerous as witchcraft, rebellion, lust and the whole spectrum of evil is — no weapon is as lethal as deception.

From the womb of deception flows all other evils. The outer work of the devil is seduction. The inner work of the devil is deception. If Satan can deceive, and deception is essentially a spiritual operation, then he can darken, and the fruition of deception and darkness is destruction. The ultimate aim of the devil is to destroy and to achieve this the subtlety of the enemy is revealed. His effort to deceive and darken is total.

There are three scriptures that speak of deception and unmask Satan's perverted attempt to abort God's plan for your life.

1. "Be not deceived, God is not mocked what so ever a man sows, that shall he also reap!" The plan of the devil is to lead humanity into a place of sowing to the flesh. Sowing to the flesh brings the corruption. The hapless and reckless attitude of sowing with words of criticism and acts of carelessness has brought much pain and remorse in the church. A man cannot sow wild oats and pray for crop failure, and this is the element of Satan's deception that has wreaked havoc in the church as renegade words have been employed by so many to level attacks against our brothers and sisters.

It is the plan of the enemy to introduce the thought that there can be sowing but that the reaping is somehow annulled or postponed. If someone can live with the belief that words are inconsequential that actions create no reaction, this takes away from life the absolute and biblical demand for circumspect living.

Sow a thought, reap an act.
Sow an act, reap a habit.
Sow a habit, reap character.

Sow character, reap destiny.
Sow destiny, reap eternity.

The devil has tried to introduce a wave of deception under the subtle disguise that life has no reaping phase so that one is not accountable to the future but certain law of reaping. Consider the following examples of sowing and reaping:

i. Jacob sowed the seeds of deception by pretending to be Esau and later in his life, his father-in-law, Laban, deceived him by giving him Leah to be his wife instead of Rachel.

ii. Abraham allowed Hagar to come into his tent, had intimate contact and Ishmael was born. Ishmael became the progenitor of the Arab population, that has created conflict with the Jews, Abraham's descendants for centuries.

iii. Moses struck the rock twice in disobedience to God's command, sowed the seed of anger and was not allowed to enter the Promised Land.

iv. David sowed the seed of deception, murder, adultery, lost the son produced by his marriage to Bathsheba, and his family was shaken for years. What ever is produced by alliances of deception will not live in the presence of God.

v. Peter sowed seeds of deception, lying and pretense, and the result was denying that he knew Jesus and the loneliness that ensued as he wept in the garden.

The scripture abounds with examples of the law of sowing and reaping and the absolutely vital importance of guarding our thoughts, words, attitudes and actions because they are all a part of the sowing and reaping cycle. If the devil can introduce the lie that life has no reaping implications, then he has brought into your life one of the greatest deceptions and this goes back to Genesis 3 when Adam found out that renegade disobedience will take you out of God's perfect plan

2. The second scripture that defines this deception is found in I John 1:8 which says, "If we say that we have no sin, we deceive ourselves, and the truth is not in us." We are not sinners because we sin, we sin because WE ARE SINNERS. There is a nature of sin within that produces actions of sin without. There is a factory of sin within that manufactures products of sin without.

This "I" nature is daily crucified by the power of the cross. So Paul speaks with exclamation, "I DIE DAILY." If we say we have no sin, then this sin principle is alive with all its venom and death. The flesh remains unchecked and uncrucified and life is now completely inundated with all the operations of the flesh as seen in Galatians 5:19-21. This is the second part of subtle deception and as is evident, this is a spiritual operation that spills over into the natural realm. If we say we have no sin then dependence on God, the blood to cleanse, the cross to crucify, the grave to bury, the resurrection to give life, and Pentecost to give power are eradicated. It is this independence and infatuation with the self life that has caused so much division, chaos, and pain in the United States. In addition, society with its emphasis on humanism, secularism and materialism has only intensified the problem. Satan thus duplicates his independence or the five "I wills" of Isaiah 14:12-15 that resulted in his banishment from heaven. For Satan to reproduce that venomous power, that vitriolic hatred, he must deceive man into self-dependence.

In this stranglehold of deception the truth is not in us, so we become consumed and swallowed by a lie, and our lives are now lost in the maze of darkness and the environment of bondage because only the truth can set you free.

3. The third scripture that addresses the issue of deception is found in James 1:22 which says, "But be ye doers of the word, and not hearers only, deceiving your own selves." This is one of Satan's primary weapons against the child of God. If he can cause someone to be only a hearer, but never translate that hearing into doing then the hearer has only been informed, not transformed. The seven messages to the churches of Revelation chapter two and three all contain the Word, "He that hath and ear, let him hear. We must not only hear with the outer ear, we must hear with the inner ear also. The physical inner ear creates balance so when you hear with the inner ear of the Spirit transformation takes place that gives balance to life (Romans 12:1,2).

However when the believer hears and never does he is inducted into the school of deception. Hearing and not doing creates a false sense of security and the position of "not doing" is exactly the plan of the enemy for the end-time. When we do what we hear, possess what we profess, walk what we talk and be what we say, a dynamic of obedience to God is created that brings release.

The woeful lack of personal witnessing and evangelism is a testimony to the fact that many hear, but do not act, and this is the paralyzing plan that Satan would establish. In these closing hours of time we as Spirit sought, blood bought, Word taught people must with holy fervor establish God's plan and purposes.

The popular definition of deception has been in itself a source of great deception. Many perceive deception to be bowing to false gods made of stone and brick yet it is clear that this outer form of deception is only a result of an inner condition. The subtly of inner deception is seen in I Timothy chapter four where the Bible speaks of seducing spirits and doctrines of devils. This is a complete prophetic unmasking of the enemy's plan in the end of time to get you to depart from the faith. So this drive of deception causes men and women to leave or apostasize from the faith given to us.

I Timothy 4 speaks of doctrines of devils. There are three of these doctrines that pervade the atmosphere of this satanic system, the doctrine of the Nicolaitanes, the doctrine of Balaam, and the doctrine of Jezebel.

1. The Doctrine of the Nicolaitanes (Revelation 2:15)
    Nike = victory, *laos*=people.
This group endeavored to recreate the hierarchy of the Old Testament priesthood to establish a priestly authority over the people. They attempted to elevate themselves into a special class of priesthood over the other Christians. They sought the sole right to interpret the scriptures for others. They were the people conquerors. Centuries later, after Constantine's conversion, this Nicolaitan heresy produced the Babylonian hierarchy of priests, leading to the spiritual dark ages of the Medieval Period.

2. The Doctrine of Balaam (Revelation 3:14)
He was hired by the kings of the Midianites and Moabites to curse the children of Israel. Balaam was a prophet who said he could influence the gods for or against men. He ran a wholesale business in favors. He advised Balak to corrupt Israel by tempting them to sin through

intermarriage, and then get the men into idol worship. These women would draw them to pagan altars, offer sacrifices to demons, make them partake of demonic things, then their impact and testimony would be lost. The doctrine is to intermarry with the world, get involved in idol worship, and defile the separation by seduction, causing you to abandon your call. We are surrounded by a world that continually offers sensuality, temptation, and is constantly trying to cause men to succumb to its influence, or enter into false worship and abandon the call.

3.   The Doctrine of Jezebel (Revelation 3: 20-22)

The worst apostasy in Israel occurred when Jezebel introduced idolatry among God's people, causing the prophets to be slain. She is the leading figure in the pageant of apostasy. Ahab married Jezebel and built pagan temples and altars (I Kings 16:33). He did more to provoke the Lord to anger by trying to make Baal the national god. Jezebel wanted Naboth's vineyard, but he would not give it. She wrote false letters in the name of the King, lied and deceived until Naboth was stoned. She called herself a prophetess, and by Ahab's choice, she occupied the Throne of Israel. Her pretense at religious leadership was in line with her character, and her voracious appetite to kill, persecute, rob, control and manipulate the servants of God. She took the seal of the King and used it, so that her level of authority would be beyond question.

These are the kinds of influences that will be prevalent in a system that denies the truth of the Word. They must be identified, dealt with and overcome.

Let's examine the birth of the church as well as the contrast between her and the surrounding society. The church was born in the womb of persecution; through pressure her enemies tried to bury her beyond the hope of resurrection. She was birthed into a Roman society where they warned her apostles not to mention the name of Jesus. Formed in the shadow of the cross where Jesus was crucified, her attackers sought to brand the memory of Christ with infamy. However, so powerful was the life and memory of Christ, the church flourished. Her members were forbidden to call Jesus "Lord" because Caesar was lord, and the Roman society that worshipped many gods through banquets and orgies viewed the fledgling church, which worshipped only one God with contempt and hatred. The Roman Empire believed in power and domination; the church believed in love.

The contrasts are so amazing yet the church came forth from the fire of persecution to shine like gold. When attacked from the outside, the gospel spread into Asia Minor and other parts of the world. Polycarp, a second century bishop of Smyrna and a martyr himself, said the blood of the martyrs became the seed of the church. The attempt to extinguish the flame of Christianity at the beginning failed miserably. The devil couldn't kill the church when the church was a baby. Do you think he has the power now that the church is 2,000 years old? Absolutely not! The church outlasted, not just survived persecution and was blessed in the midst of it. The church's survival, nay its flourishing growth, from the all-out attack against it, defines it as a spiritual superpower. Only something supernatural could have survived, after the enemy leveled such a unified, unrelenting attack against this infant church.

The historical tracing of secular leadership and those opposed to Christ produces an interesting pattern of self-extinction. When Nebuchadnezzar and Belshazzar died, Babylon died. When Xerxes died, the Persian Empire began to fall apart. When Alexander the Great died, the Grecian Empire began to disintegrate. When the ten emperors of Rome died, Rome was splintered into the many countries of Europe. When Hitler died, the Third Reich died. When Napoleon died, the Napoleonic crusades died. These governments died when their heroes died, because the fate of the empire resided in one man, a human with human frailty. The man was the life, the power, and the support line for the movement. When he died, the movement died!

In contrast, the history of church leadership clearly depicts the biblical principle of life from death. John 12:24 states, "I tell you the truth, unless a kernel of wheat falls to the ground and dies, it remains a single seed. But if it dies, it produces many seeds."

When Mark died at Alexandria after being dragged through the city, the church didn't die. When John was boiled in oil, escaped death, and was exiled to Patmos, the church didn't die. When Peter was crucified at Rome (upside down because he refused to be crucified in the same way his Lord had been), the church didn't die. When James, the brother of John, was beheaded at Jerusalem, the church didn't die. When the other James was tossed from the pinnacle of the temple and beaten to death, the church didn't die. When Andrew was bound to a cross and preached until he was dead, the church didn't die. When Thomas was run through with a lance, the church didn't die. When Jude was shot with arrows, the church didn't die. When Matthias was stoned and beheaded, the church didn't die. When Barnabas was stoned at Salonica, the church didn't die. When Paul was beheaded in Rome, the church didn't die.

WHY? Because the life of the church is not in the apostle, the prophet, the evangelist, the teacher, the preacher or the super hero. There is only one hero in the church and only one lifeline of power and glory, his name is Jesus Christ, the Son of the Living God whose I am and whom I serve. Therein lies the indestructibility of the church. Therein lies the glory, the power, and the eternality of the body of Christ.

This hero is found in each and every believer and together we will accomplish the prophetic plan for America based on the Founding Father's faith in Almighty God. He is not finished with us yet. The church is not a country club where rituals are sacred. It's not a political action group or a pressure block of idealists. It is not a religious democracy. The church is the expressed will and prophetic plan of God in America, from its inception. The uncompromising, blood-bought church is indestructible!

Israel was attacked by the Midianites and we in America are attacked by the MEDIA-ITES. The media has done its best to convince the believers that they are powerless in the system as it now exists. How wrong they are! The attacks upon the church have been abundant and from every possible direction, but the church rises because the life of the church is not in the blood of the preacher or the ability of the preacher or the eloquence of the super star. It is in the power, glory and resurrection life of Jesus Christ. He is still alive! No wonder Jesus said, "Blessed are you, Simon son of Jonah, for this was not revealed to you by man, but by my Father in heaven. And I tell you that you are Peter, and on this rock I will build my church, and the gates of Hades will not overcome it. I will give you the keys of the kingdom of heaven; whatever you bind on earth will be bound in heaven, and whatever you loose on earth will be loosed in heaven" (Matthew 16:17-19).

There is something in the church so powerful that when the enemy comes against it he has no power to dissolve the glory of the living Christ within its vessels. When we look at the above verse we see God's strategy: "Upon this rock" is the foundation, "I will build" is the formation and fellowship, "the gates of Hades will not overcome it" is the future endurance, and "whatever you bind on earth will be bound in heaven" is the function for the church. The church cannot and never will be destroyed. It is a supernatural divine creation of God. Not only has it survived its attackers, its martyred saints, it has spread, it has increased, it has been blessed, it has been lifted and it has the power.

There are many opinions about the position of America in the Bible. I will give some of these opinions for your general information.

1. Revelation 12:14: Some say that the great eagle mentioned here is a reference to America, but this text seems to be speaking of the speed with which the woman, (Israel) flees into the wilderness to escape the persecution of the Antichrist.

2. Isaiah 18:1: Some say that the land shadowed with wings beyond the river of Ethopia is America. Verse two speaks of a nation scattered and peeled, meted (measured) out trodden down, whose land the rivers have spoiled. Many point to the fact that America is a vast expanse measured out in states and cities and feel this is a parallel to Isaiah measuring out in this verse.

3. Ezekiel 38:13: There are yet some that see a reference to America with the merchants of Tarshish and "The Young Lions." Tarshish is mentioned 20 times in the Bible. The International Bible Encyclopedia says, This is a reference to Britain. For the word "merchants" the explanation is given that there was only one way to trade then and that was by ships. The slogan was, Britannia rules the waves and England, the mistress of the seas.

4. Jeremiah 50; 51: There are many that see these chapters as a reference to America, so by virtue of their interpretation Babylon and America are synonymous terms!

Now here is a thought. You can push a nuclear trigger and you can devastate a nation. You can press a missile button and you can obliterate a town. But, when you have the greatest weapon on the face of the earth, the gospel of Jesus Christ, and preach it to a nation, that whole nation can be changed and saved by the power of God. When Russia fell in basically one day, what was the immediate request to America? Send us your missionaries we want to hear the gospel.

John F. Kennedy was killed on November 22, 1963. Had he lived his next speech would have contained the following, "We in this country, in this generation, are—by destiny rather than choice—the watchmen on the walls of world freedom. We ask, therefore, that we may be worthy of our power and responsibility, that we may exercise our strength with wisdom and restraint, and that we may achieve in our time and for all time the ancient vision of peace on earth, goodwill toward men. That must always be our goal....For as was written long ago, "Except the

Lord keep the city, the watchman waketh but in vain" (Psalm 127:1b).

America has been prepared for this great visitation of God. The church has been prepared for the harvest. The greatest "hero" the world has ever known is getting ready to split the sky, and every eye shall behold him.

These nations that are accepting the false religion of the world are trying to influence you in America to join with them. These are the kinds of influences that will be prevalent in a system that denies the truth of the Word. They must be identified, dealt with and overcome. Here are some practical things we can do to navigate this sea of evil and be conquerors, and be able to help others that have been snared by these religious traps:

1. We must never compromise our belief system for the sensational touch of the world.
2. We must be ready to have an unconditional commitment to the King.
3. We must be not only informed, but personally transformed by the power of the Word.
4. We must have God's power, and God's Spirit flowing in us as we deal with the antichrist systems.
5. We must be a beacon to those who are succumbing; we must be an example of all that we believe.

Your belief is your life. What you believe influences how you behave. Don't fumble the ball church! We have a prophetic destiny to fulfill!

Chapter Four

The Prophetic Assignment
Found In The
Seed

There is something unique and miraculous about the inception of America's government. From its very beginning this government has been based upon two major principles: the acknowledgment of a sovereign God and man's responsibility before God. These two principles are so tightly woven into the fabric of this Republic that their removal would destroy its capacity to function properly. Our government functions best on the principle that God is the ultimate authority and that all men, including our national leadership, are ultimately accountable to him. Beloved, it has never been easy for Christians in America. The Puritans faced the same challenges that we face today. Man is a sinner and needs the saving grace of Jesus Christ to become holy, honorable and useful in the kingdom of God.

America's history is unique among the other nations of the modern world. Of course this statement evokes an unpopular sentiment in a generation that hears much about a global community. This mind-set is what I call the "one-worldness." The antichrist spirit that prevails in the world today feels it must break down all the political barriers and make us citizens of this New World Order. We are not to be identified as Americans. In order to enter into the New World Order, the global community's national barriers of sovereignty must be torn down.

In the deluded attempt to govern himself apart from God man has endeavored to actualize his potential for genius and wickedness and has essentially brought this world and its system economically, politically, socially and militarily to the edge of disaster.

Now the secular lords of lunacy have seen the consequences of their excesses as global famine, environmental disaster, the possibility of nuclear war, economic recession in many places ravage our world. The disintegration of the social fabric has become a firm unavoidable reality. The New World Order has found reason for being, as it postulates its foundational principle that if the world is UNITED in its effort for peace, if it takes care of the environment, if it opposes terrorism and dictators, reverses social disintegration along with community participation the world will enter a new phase of a new world hitherto unknown. The complication is that the international structure will be cast into this mold and that nations will relate to one another in a new way and this declaration of the leaders of our world.

This syncretism of nations, beliefs, ideologies and the surrender of authority to a supra national body includes military, political, religious and economic elements. This New World Order subsequently weaves a fabric of control around all the systems that the world functions by. When one understands the all-inclusive plan and the commandeering of every system to make the bigger picture possible, there is a remarkable and profound parallel to Genesis 11. This New World Order is only a repetition of what was attempted several millennia ago in Babylon when humanity exhibited the greatest display of unity in the history of the world.

Genesis 11:4 states that the purpose of this united demonstration was to construct a tower whose top would reach unto heaven. In their attempt to transcend physical limitations they were reaching not into but unto heaven, giving the emphasis that the Babel builders had launched a project using the latest technology of their day with the religion of human deification producing a deadly combination.

The ultimate aim is the godhead of man as he plays the game of Russian roulette with his soul and his eternal future. The unity on every front today is but a duplicate of this Babel project and by glorifying human pride, by advocating self sufficiency, rather than advocating dependence on God and His Word the political, religious, economical, military fraternity will soon hear the sound of a mighty crash with incalculable consequences. What is considered New is actually a revival of the age-old foundation and plan that has been exposed as a failed attempt from a self created universal brotherhood. The aim is to bring about some millennium of peace and order. Its destiny is failure as seen in Genesis 11.

A variety of opinions have always emerged from within this country. We look at abortion and see it ripping the conscience of the nation apart. Slavery did the same thing in the 1800s. The issues change but the power to heal and come to truth will always be found in the local church. One small group committed to righteousness for the sake of Christ can change the world. Are we willing to pay the price? That is the question.

The seed of the gospel that was planted in America contains all the character attributes this country's laws were built upon. It is a principle of nature that the character of a thing develops according to the nature of its seed. That has not changed. The Declaration of Independence, The Bill of Rights and The Constitution all have their foundation in the Gospels of the Bible and the Torah (the five books of Moses). The final sentence of The Declaration of Independence contains a declaration of dependence on Almighty God. From the Mayflower Compact of November 19, 1620 to The Declaration of Independence, the name of God and Christian principles are inextricably woven into the fabric of these documents of governance.

We must not cower in fear and trepidation as we see agnostics, atheists, and secular humanism stage their drama to replace the foundation upon which this country was formed and its principles founded.

There is a prophetic guarantee of Matthew 16:18,19 where God himself will be the one that builds the church. In two verses the prophetic destiny of the church, the body of Christ is revealed and the assurance of a glorious tomorrow is given. There is a divine foundation, a holy formation, a sweet fellowship, a certain destiny and an awesome function all given to the church. It is in this context that we go back to see the original plan and intent of the forefathers of America. The clear design seen is that God truly ordained this nation to be a place of freedom in His Word, and proclamation of His Word and living by His Word. Of all the national documents of countries around the world, there is none that reveals such an emphasis on Biblical principles.

A tremendous assignment has been given to the Christian, to the church and to this country. The enemy is endeavoring to destroy this nation because of its prophetic assignment, to be the church and export the gospel for the glory of God.

It is here that Satan's greatest prophetic attack on America is seen. The attack is not on the economic system, the political system or the military system. No, this demonic attack against America is on the spirit of the God-fearing people of America. In the fifties we saw a healthy respect for basic moral principles of the true church of Jesus Christ. The television shows were, I Love Lucy, Lassie, Leave it to Beaver, Andy Griffith and many more. These shows carried a respect for the Judeo-Christian values of that day. The family was a basic unit of love, care, support and Mom and Dad married and were in love with each other.

Today, the perversion is pumped into our homes by NYPD Blue, Roseanne, Beverly Hills 90210, talk shows, Friends, and the list goes on and on. These shows come complete with profanity, nakedness, drunkenness, and sexual acts imitated, leaving nothing to the imagination. There is a mocking of Judeo-Christian ethics and the false doctrine and antichrist spirit spills into millions of American homes daily. Pornography is now the third most profitable business in America.

Humanity has always had its moral lapses. Greece worshipped sex. Rome had the destructive lust of the flesh. Sparta sported its pride on homosexuality. Yet, there has always been a remnant of people that has registered a repulsion of this abnormal, perverted lifestyle, and called for a return to moral purity. Today, the cry for repentance is almost gone. The alarm at deviance and the shock over immorality is almost non-existent. 2 Timothy 3:1-5 says, "This know also, that in the last days perilous times shall come. For men shall be lovers of their own selves, covetous, boasters, proud, blasphemers, disobedient to parents, unthankful, unholy, without natural affection, trucebreakers, false accusers, incontinent fierce despisers of those that are good, Traitors, heady, high-minded, lovers of pleasures more than lovers of God; Having a form of godliness, but denying the power thereof: from such turn away."

There are some characteristics that will become lifestyles in the world and will be tattooed on mankind by the spirit of the antichrist. The purpose of this spirit is threefold:

1. To make the abnormal seem normal, so that when the antichrist makes all his abnormal claims, they will be readily accepted.
2. To saturate the earth with this spirit so minds will be desensitized to evil and this way, evil will become acceptable.
3. To introduce another system or scale of values so that your life will be judged by that value system instead of the Word of God.

There is a rebellion in dress, morals, music, literature, behavior, families, and now even in the church life. When men live the life of the "I will," they are trying to take the place of the "I AM." Rebellion against the pastor, the Word, and God's authority are all the same. This must be identified as Satan's attempt to desolate and desecrate this temple. We must deal with this problem of carnal indulgence, intellectual acceptance without spiritual revival, and opposition to the things of God. So many are trapped in the tentacles of rebellion and they feel like they are just acting in accordance with human nature. I can assure you that this is a trap to damn your soul and desecrate your temple! The New Age movement has offered no apology for making a bold and convincing statement of its belief system through the entertainment and media frenzy of the world. Because of the religious and deceptive nature of the New Age movement and its universal acceptance, many Christians have become unwittingly ensnared, by its duplicate doctrines and beliefs.

But, there is the sound in the wind of those starting to rise up and say, "Enough is enough." It is a faint cry, but one that is being heard and seen in the pockets of revival starting to spring up in unique cities of America. Think about this, the leaders of fifteen former Soviet states are begging American Christians to bring Bibles, to teach them how to pray and show them the principles of Christianity. When the Berlin Wall fell, Eastern Europe cried out for Bibles and missionaries to teach the word and help establish churches. This is the cry of the world to America!

They recognize the seed that was planted here and the success of its growth. Now they are begging us to plant their fields. We dare not fail and we dare not disintegrate from within. The facade of the enemy dare not blind us. Yes, there is danger in this country, but it must not rob the country of its true identity. It is no wonder all the attacks can be traced back to a singular attack on the basic, fundamental character of the true uncompromised church of Jesus Christ.

Each day Americans are forced to undergo an insidious form of mental and social shock as they turn on the television set. Each day they become more numb as they watch the accounts of mass murders, husbands killing wives, wives maiming husbands, children killing children, sports figures going to jail, and the clergy being brought before the public to be ridiculed, mocked and jailed. We see the ravages of the drug lords and the drug pushers in our own families and feel paralyzed against the onslaught.

Are we being purposely desensitized and anesthetized? Is something happening to take away the assignment of prophecy in this country? Yes, the antichrist system has a plan. America's prophetic assignment is not to be the world's policeman, the world's benefactor, or world's deliverer. America's prophetic plan is plain and simple. It is to win the lost to Jesus Christ before that great and dreadful day of Armageddon and to be a shield and cover for the nation of Israel.

Is they are some organized attempt of the enemy to so attack righteousness, and so blind and influence us that the church becomes powerless, her effectiveness blunted? The major attacks in this country are precisely directed against Biblical principles and the church of Jesus Christ.

The devil disguised as an angel of light has leveled this intense attack to inoculate the nation against the Word of God and the purposes of God. The inevitable result—dependency on the enemy's belief system. Continuing belief in the enemy's system will lead inexorably to a downward spiral. It is precisely this kind of onslaught that caused John the Baptist to declare that there must be a turning from this Satanic infiltration and a returning to Godly and absolute values.

If the church will not rise to the challenge, it will leave an open door for Satan's diabolical domination that will be energized by seducing spirits and doctrines of devils. Christians must therefore, arise to defy this Satanic onslaught of counterfeit beliefs and uphold with honor the Bible beliefs and doctrines.

2 Thessalonians 2:1-5 reads, "Now we beseech you, brethren, by the coming of our Lord Jesus Christ, and by

our gathering together unto him, that ye be not soon shaken in mind, or be troubled neither by spirit, nor by word, nor by letter as from us, as that the day of Christ is at hand. Let no man deceive you by any means: for that day shall not come, except there come a falling away first, and that man of sin be revealed, the son of perdition; Who opposeth and exalteth himself above all that is called God, or that is worshipped; so that he as God sitteth in the temple of God, shewing himself that he is God. Remember ye not, that, when I was yet with you, I told you these things?"

If he can continue to numb us into a twilight sleep, where we focus on the negative elements, we will never awaken to our greatness and power found in the gospel of Jesus Christ! We cannot let him prevail against us.

Ask yourself, "Where is the greatness in this country?" It is not in Washington, the economy, the military or prosperity, but it is found in each individual soul filled with the Spirit of the Living God. The power to change this country and impact the world in the greatest end-time harvest is found in you, the uncompromised child of a living God. Scripture is clear and tells us that God will judge his own house first. We have seen that happen over the past several years. God is saying clearly, "Time is up!"

Judgment will do either of two things. It will either harden your heart like it hardened Pharaoh's or it will cause you to turn back to a right way. Five years ago I preached that the American church would begin to rise. She would begin to be intolerant of sin, compromise and mediocrity. A remnant would be raised up. It is important to remember God usually works from the minority to the majority not the majority to the minority. He usually moves from the in to the out, not from the out to the in. He starts with a remnant and ends with a multitude. God is beginning to do something miraculous in the church. We must get our eyes and ears focused on what the Spirit of God is saying, not the late-night news anchorman. We have been planted by God himself and when we spring forth, the character of the seed will look like Jesus.

The tide is just now faintly beginning to turn in America. Schools are pressing for prayer to be reinstated. Hundreds of thousands of young people are beginning to make commitments of abstinence. People are beginning to see that free sex has a tremendous price tag attached to it. I believe with Desert Storm we saw the beginning of a tremendous prayer revival, as churches were open twenty-four hours a day. The Bible is very clear concerning the connection between prayer and a nation. It says:"...if my people, who are called by my name, will humble themselves and pray and seek my face and turn from their wicked ways, then I will hear from heaven and will forgive their sin and will heal their land. Now my eyes will be open and my ears attentive to the prayers offered in this place" (II Chronicles 7:14).

God has always dealt with his people first and then the world. It is an Old Testament maxim; if you want to judge Sodom you have got to talk to Lot first. I believe when God allowed America to be in Desert Storm it so tugged at the hearts of her citizens that they went back to God and prayed. It was the silence and the self-sufficiency of the church that originally cut off the flow; the "I have need of nothing" attitude. The, I can go to church as if it were some social club; the, I can be filled, as if it were a gas station attitude.

Listen carefully America, the church is not a reservoir where you fill up; it is a place where you become a channel so the power of God can flow through you! You are not a reservoir you are a conduit. Church, you are beginning to stir. I am seeing this all over the country. I am seeing a return to the basics and what worked in the past. Again, if you want to understand the character of something, go back to its seed. The seed of America came from and was planted by the hand of God.

Why has the enemy tried to cause this country to deivate from God's prophetic plan? Because it is the most powerful plan on earth. As we saw when people prayed during Desert Storm, the war was miraculously over in forty days. Like Nineveh after forty days of prayer and fasting, the country turned around. America is beginning to see results from that prayer of forty days.

If God's people will continue to pray, preach, and become diligent, the Spirit of God will come and set their vessels on fire for the gospel. This is happening in hundreds of churches in America, and is producing a rippling effect. I believe prayer produces an earthquake in the spirit realm, which, in turn, shakes the world. The world is shaking now. We have the promise of God that everywhere the soles of our feet touch is given to us.

America, how precious are the feet of those you have sent to the nations who carry the good news of Jesus. You have planted much and now the season of harvest has come. The harvest of righteousness found within your shores contains the power and the character of Jesus. America, the church within your midst embodies what the world desperately needs. It's time! Go and sow the seed!

Chapter Five

Prophetic Coincidence?

We often look to Columbus as the man who discovered America. Let's look at an excerpt from his diary, "It was the Lord who put it in my mind. I could feel His hand upon me. There is no question that the inspiration was from the Holy Spirit, because He comforted me with rays of illumination from the Holy Scriptures. It was simply a fulfillment of what Isaiah had prophesied. The fact that the gospel must be preached to so many lands. No one should fear to undertake a task in the name of the Savior if it is just and if the intention is purely for His service and His alone."

America it's a land of majestic hills and lush green valleys, it's a country of tall skyscrapers and mile-high cities, it's a place of technological advances and creative people. "Give me your tired, give me your poor, your huddled masses yearning to breathe free," counsels the Statue of Liberty as she holds out her torch to light the way for the thousands who come from around the world. The statue is a symbol of hope to the world. God ordained that America would be the container of that hope.

On October 28,1886, the celebration and dedication of the Statute of Liberty began with a prayer from Reverend Richard S. Storrs, D. D.: "Almighty God, our Heavenly Father, who art of infinite majesty and mercy, by whose counsel and might the courses of the worlds are wisely ordained and irresistibly established, yet who takest thought of the children of men, and to whom our homage in all our works is justly due: We bless and praise Thee....

It is in Thy favor, and through the operation the Gospel of Thy grace, that cities stand in quiet prosperity; that peaceful commerce covers the seas....

We pray that the Liberty, which it represents, may continue to enlighten with beneficent instruction, and to bless with majestic and wide benediction, the nations, which have part in this work of renown....

We pray for all the nations of the earth; that in equity and charity their sure foundations may be established; that in piety and wisdom they may find a true welfare, in obedience to Thee, glory and praise; and that, in all the enlargements of their power, they may be ever the joyful servants of Him to whose holy dominion and kingdom shall be no end...." [1].

There can be no denying that the world has looked to America for its spiritual guidance, protection, mercy and grace. America has become the melting pot of the world because of this favor from God.

The governments of the world seem to be meshing at tremendous speed. Everywhere you turn you hear the term, New World Order. The order is purported to be all in the name of freedom and democracy. This great new government is supposed to transcend national priorities and make the world a safer place.

One of the major reasons God has so blessed this country financially is that America has given so much to the world. America is still the number one country of the world in spreading the gospel of Jesus Christ. The church has been given the designated privilege to be the watchmen on the wall in the end-time. Eighty-five percent of all world missions and evangelism comes from the church in America. **It is clear God is not going to silence the very instrument he created to be the gift to the world.**

Most nations have very strict banking controls concerning sending money to other nations. As an American citizen you can basically bank anywhere you want in the world. It is a free option. America is also one of the few countries of the world whose citizens are allowed to give sizable amounts of money to the church and count them as tax deductions.

America has been given a tremendous prophetic assignment and it will not be finished until the church is caught up in the rapture and taken away. Until that time she has been given the dynamic role of standing as a friend to Israel, with strength and power to back up her position as a true support. God has promised to bless those who bless Israel. Isaiah 40:1-2 says, "Comfort ye, comfort ye my people, saith your God. Speak ye comfortably to Jerusalem, and cry unto her, that her warfare is accomplished, that her iniquity is pardoned: for she hath received of the Lord's hand double for all her sins. The voice of him that crieth in the wilderness, 'Prepare ye the way of the Lord, make straight in the desert a highway for our God.'"

The true uncompromised church is Israel's greatest ally. We must realize that the strength of the church is its ability to influence the world to deal with Israel in peace. America is like a loving father given the assignment of support and protection of Israel. There is no other nation on the face of the earth that Israel can really count on except America. As long as the church is alive in America she will exist to fulfill this God-given prophetic responsibility.

America WAKE UP! I would like to show you why America has suffered this past 12 years from natural disasters. We have not kept the prophetic assignment to protect, nurture and help Israel to the extent that scriptures demand of us. I would like to give you a list and I do believe when you have finished reading this section of the book you will have to say that these facts are overwhelming evidence and not JUST A COINCIDENCE! Genesis 12:3 states, "I will bless those who bless you, and whoever curses you I will curse; and all peoples on earth will be blessed through you." If we stand with Israel we will continue to be a blessed nation, if we go against Israel we will be doomed.

1. October 30, 1991 President George Bush convened the Middle East Peace Plan in Madrid, Spain. The purpose was for Israel to be convinced to give up land for the peace process. The Bible clearly states that Israel is in a covenant with God for this land. The same day we were saying, "Give up the promise" a ferocious storm hit the New England states called, "The Perfect Storm." Meteorologist said it was one of the most powerful storms ever to occur. A book and a very successful movie were made and showed how terrible this storm really was. There had never been anything like it before.

2. August 23, 1992 The Madrid Peace Conference moved to Washington, D.C. and the talks resumed. Again, we were asking Israel to break the covenant of the Promised Land. Again, the same day Hurricane Andrew hit Florida. Hurricane Andrew

hit Florida with such a force that people, homes, businesses and life in many areas would never be the same again.

3. September 1, 1993 secret negotiations were going on to get Israel to agree to give away Gaza and Jericho to the Palestinians. Again, on the same day Hurricane Emily crawled across the Atlantic Ocean and hit North Carolina with 115-mile hour winds.

4. January 16, 1994 President Clinton met with Syria's President Hafez Assad and they discussed a plan that would force Israel to give up the Golan Heights. Within twenty-four hours the United States was rocked with a devastating earthquake in California. The Northridge quake was devastating. The damage in dollars was staggering.

5. March 1, 1997 Yasser Arafat arrived in Washington to meet with President Clinton. Arafat was upset about the building of thousands of home in East Jerusalem. Clinton and Arafat discussed a way of being able to announce Palestinian statehood and divide Jerusalem. Again, the same day powerful tornadoes devastated many parts of the nation. Storms caused tremendous flooding. Most of the storms caused well over one billion dollars in damage. These storms carried well into April and the worst storms in a century were recorded in the Dakotas.

6. July 15, 1997 The United Nations made a resolution to boycott Israeli products to punish

them for building in Jerusalem. That very same week the nation's stock markets were shaken. Asia's stock market plummeted and Brazil was extremely hard hit.

7. January 21, 1998 Prime Minister Benjamin Netanyahu met with Clinton. Again they were pressuring Netanyahu to give up the covenant Promised Land. When this meeting ended Clinton was openly revealed to be involved with Monica Lewinsky. The sex scandal was now public and during this time impeachment was talked about. Before the year would be over Clinton would have two articles of impeachment that would go all the way to the Senate for a trial.

8. Sept 27, 1998 Clinton met with the leaders Arafat and Netanyahu in the White House and the consensus was that Israel was to sign and give away 13 % of her land. Around this same time, a few days before the scheduled meeting Hurricane Georges slammed into the Gulf Coast and the eye of the storm struck Mississippi and damaged Florida also. There were tremendous amounts of rain and flooding.   Again, staggering dollars in damage.

9. October 15, 1998 Clinton, Netanyahu and Arafat met at Wye Plantation, Maryland. The meetings were to last for five days and again centered on giving up 13% of the West Bank. Again, starting immediately rains and tornadoes hit and kept up their force until the end of the Middle East talks.

In the end the storms during this week alone caused over one billion dollars in damage.

10. November 30, 1998 Clinton held meetings with 42 nations and Arafat. Arafat wanted America to give her the $400 million Clinton was promising and $1.7 billion from the other nations. The purpose was to help Palestine to announce statehood with Jerusalem as its capital. Again, as the meetings were going on, the American stock market dropped 216 points in one day. Within two days the European markets fell an economic disaster in Europe. America was in an extremely dangerous position one we are still recovering from in terms of the stock market. We were putting our fist in the face of God and assuming we had the authority over Jerusalem.

11. March 23, 1999 Arafat met with Clinton again to discuss the issue of Palestinian statehood and Jerusalem as the capital. Again, the very same day our stock market took its biggest fall in months. The next day Clinton called for the attack on Serbia. That same week, Maryland's governor, Parris Glending gave approval and banned discrimination based on sexual orientation and same sex unions.

12. May 3, 1999 Arafat was declaring a Palestinian state with Jerusalem as its capital. Again, the same day the most powerful tornado ever to hit America smashed down in Oklahoma and Kansas with winds of over 300 miles per hour. Total damage was in the billions (plural) dollars.

13. September 1, 1999 Madeleine Albright met with Arab leaders and Prime Minister Ehud Barak. The issue for Israel was give up the land! Again, on the very day, Hurricane Floyd hit the United States. Storms hit North Carolina and 18,000 square miles were destroyed. The stock market plunged and an earthquake shook three states. As the Jewish settlers were being forced to move, the stock market fell, the West Coast had an earthquake and the East Coast was hit by a hurricane. Coincidence?

14. January 4, 2000 Ehud Barak, Farouk al-Shara, of Syria and Clinton meet to convince Israel to give up the Golan Heights, which is a tremendous piece of property for the military defense of Israel. Again, on the very same day the stock market hit with the worst drop ever in our history. The combined monetary losses for this one-day were over $600 billion.

15. July 12-26, 2000 Clinton was at Camp David, Maryland in meetings with Arafat and Barak. Again, that very week of meetings forest fires began to erupt in the West and burned out of control well into the month of August. Entire states were declared disaster areas.

America as you can see this is almost out of the realm of the possibility for chance. This is the divine intervention of an Almighty God who is clearly saying, "I will bless those who bless Israel and curse those who don't." We need to make a decision church. We need to get very vocal and express our commitment and dedication to the Word of God and Israel! Zechariah 2:8 says about Israel, "This is what the Lord Almighty says, 'He sent me against the nations that have plundered you-for-whoever touches you touches the apple of his eye...'" Again, in Zechariah 12:9 it says, "On that day I will set out to destroy all the nations that attack Jerusalem."

The media would like to convince you that Americans are hated and loathed around the world but that is just not true. Consider how the inhabitants of Grenada responded when Reagan sent troops to their island. Signs of thanksgiving were placed on the walls and shouts of "God bless you" were heard over the microphones from grateful hearts due to America's intervention. If God were going to destroy America how could he answer all the millions of prayers of believers, from all over the world, who are praising him for the church in America and its generosity?

The media works constantly to silence positive reports on America. You will never hear about the prosperity of the church or the goodwill being produced by it. Instead, the media stresses the rebellion and the bad news. The devil has targeted this nation. He wants to ruin it, close down the churches, take away the tax benefits, raise up persecution against the ministries, corrupt from within, batter from without and, if all that fails, make the church unaware of and apathetic to its supernatural position in America.

What is the answer to the attack of Satan? Preachers must sound the call for a revival of righteousness and holiness in the church. We must renew our vows of commitment to Israel and the lost. God has blessed America so she can bless the world!

Chapter Six

Israel And The Church
Vs. The Antichrist System

Remember this: Whoever sows sparingly will also reap sparingly, and whoever sows generously will also reap generously. Each man should give what he has decided in his heart to give, not reluctantly or under compulsion, for God loves a cheerful giver. And God is able to make all grace abound to you, so that in all things at all times, having all that you need, you will abound in every good work. As it is written: "He has scattered abroad his gifts to the poor; his righteousness endures forever. Now he who supplies seed to the sower and bread for food will also supply and increase your store of seed and will enlarge the harvest of your righteousness. You will be made rich in every way so that you can be generous on every occasion, and through us your generosity will result in thanksgiving to God" (II Corinthians 9: 6-12).

This service that you perform is not only supplying the needs of God's people but is also overflowing in many expressions of thanks to God. Because of the service by which you have proved yourselves, men will praise God for the obedience that accompanies your confession of the gospel of Christ, and for your generosity in sharing with them and with everyone else. And in their prayers for you their hearts will go out to you, because of the surpassing grace God has given you. Thanks be to God for his indescribable gift! (II Corinthians (:12-15)

Christians in the United States and Canada are funding ninety-five percent (eighty-five percent of which comes from America) of missions and the gospel outreach. We are supporting the cost of world evangelism because it is the purpose and plan of God for us. The word of God is true. It states that the receiver of the gift will thank God and pray for the giver. America, as the result of this has the greatest army of prayer warriors around the world praying on her behalf. I can recall how grateful I was for my missionary friends and the support they received from America.

I am not trying to paint a perfect picture of America. I know there is much evil in this country. The United States has problems with drug use, homosexuality, pornography, promiscuity, abortion, alcoholism and violent crime. This moral decline is a result of a spiritual decline. This spiritual decline, in turn, is contributing to the social, political and economic decline in America. The answer is the true and living church of Jesus Christ waking up to its real power. Winning the lost to the saving grace of Jesus Christ and remembering our love and commitment to Israel is where the true power of the church will be seen. In an instant a reprobate can be transformed and in a prayer, standing in the gap, for Israel, God can stop the hands of time.

It is very clear in the Old Testament that God had a sovereign plan for the nation of Israel. Isaiah 45:4 calls Israel God's elect and this along with Exodus 19:5-6 where Israel is called a peculiar treasure, a kingdom of priests, a holy nation, presents to us a picture of God's plan for this nation.

In the New Testament in Romans 8:33, The church, the body of Christ is called the elect. I Peter 2:9 calls the church a royal priesthood, a holy nation and a peculiar treasure. The similarities between Israel and the Church are astonishing, yet the most devastating lie of the enemy in the realm of Bible Prophecy is when professors, teachers, with over ambitious unbalanced and highly speculative theology, teach that the church has replaced Israel. How woefully bankrupt this lie is and how it robs so many of seeing the divine connection between Israel and the church.

Even though God has sovereignly elected these two groups, their destiny and purposes are different yet their blessing is simultaneous. Gal 3:29 says, "And if ye be Christ's then ye are Abraham's seed, and heirs according to the promise." This is a phenomenal verse that opens up a spiritual world of revelation to see the connection between belonging to Christ and Abraham's seed. Galatians speaks of the blessings of Abraham coming on us through Jesus and Ephesians 2:12, "That at that time ye were without Christ, being aliens from the commonwealth of Israel, and strangers from the covenants of promise, having no hope, and without God in the world: But now in Christ Jesus ye who sometimes were far off are made nigh by the blood of Christ." This verse speaks of the estrangement from the commonwealth of Israel at that time when we were without God. Not only were we far from God, we were far from the commonwealth of Israel, so being drawn nigh now, we are inevitably placed closer to Israel. There is a divine identification between the church and Israel outlined in Romans 11:17 where we as a wild olive tree, were grafted in among them. We were joined by an act of God grafting us into this Jewish tree so we could partake of the root and the fatness of their olive tree.

Now, there is an incredible internal drive to go back to our Jewish roots as seen in the blowing of the shofar, the wearing of the prayer shawl, (tallith) and the studying of the feasts of the Lord. Herein lies another spiritual crossroads for America, one our people must understand. Whoever touches Israel for evil, touches the apple of God's eye. We are called to bless Israel because through their seed, we have become one family through Father Abraham's seed, our Savior Jesus Christ. America's true church understands that the covenant promises to Israel cannot be broken without severe results, as the list of 15, the last chapter so clearly shows.

America with Israel is standing at the crossroads of prophetic judgment or blessing. There is a prophetic fulfillment of scriptures coming that no man can stop or change. The decision, the power, and the protection of this country rests in the men and women who understand, without wavering, that what Israel has gained — the Promised Land — really came as a prophetic fulfillment. To ask her to give it up would be to challenge the living God who has sworn to act on her behalf and judge any nation that comes against this divine land of Israel.

When Israel became a nation on May 14, 1948, an entire generation, and the entire world felt the impact demographically, militarily, religiously of this singular pivotal event that was prophesied thousands of years ago.

Consider these changes that took place in 1948 just because God began moving prophetically with a nation that was scattered, beaten, blamed, killed and plundered for centuries.

1. In 1948 Kim Sung II set up the republic of North Korea which has a huge army today and adds to the instability of the Far East.

2. In 1948 Mahatma Ghandi was assassinated and
    this was a pivotal event that culminated in the
    independence of India the following year.
    Recently, India and Pakistan exploded nuclear
    weapons and their animosity to each other
    continues to be a destabilizing factor in the East.

3. Mao Tse Tung forced the Chinese government to
    flee to Taiwan in 1948 and gave birth to The
    Peoples Republic of China who now has shown its
    extreme military nature with its conflict with
    Taiwan and recent problems with America.

Revelation 16:12 speaks of the Battle of Armageddon
and the Kings of the East. We know that this eastern
military horde, a coalition of powers in the east, is now
clearly evident. Are they being prepared to be used as a
force against America should she continue on her present
course of forcing Israel to give up land for peace?

4. In 1948 The United Nations began with 66
    nations.

5. In 1948 the World Council of Churches was
    formed.

6. In 1948, *Oral Roberts and Billy Graham began
    their Crusades, changing the landscape of world
    outreach.*

With one prophecy coming to pass, the rebirth of
Israel, the world and the church were impacted like never
before, and changes occurred and are occurring because
this is the generation that was spoken of in Matthew 24
that will see all things come to pass. This is a moment of

accelerated prophetic fulfillment where God has put history in the fast-forward mode.

America, it is time to come out of the deception of this world and back to the truth of the scriptures that clearly states, "On that day I will set out to destroy all the nations that attack Jerusalem" (Zechariah 12:9), "I am going to make Jerusalem a cup that sends all the surrounding peoples reeling. Judah will be besieged as well as Jerusalem. On that day, when all the nations of the earth are gathered against her, I will make Jerusalem an immovable rock for all nations. *All* who try to move it will injure themselves" (Zechariah 12:2-3), and "So do not fear, for I am with you; do not be dismayed, for I am your God. I will strengthen you and help you; I will uphold you with my righteous right hand. All who rage against you will surely be ashamed and disgraced; those who oppose you will be as nothing and perish" (Isaiah 41:10-11).

The true church of Jesus Christ should never endorse the peace plans of the world that cut up, carve up and slice up Jerusalem or the Jewish nation of Israel. God said he was setting his throne up in Jerusalem and Jesus, himself, would rule and reign for a thousand years from that throne! Do we dare think we can change this prophetic plan of God?

There is a religious, deceptive thread that is woven into the fabric of satanic operation and it is consummated fully in the emergence of Satan's church in the Tribulation Period. No leader can mobilize a world, bring them under the umbrella of his empire on an economic, political, or military basis alone. The glue that can transcend national, racial and social boundaries is religion.

The antichrist will succeed because of this religious power. August 28 through September 5, 1993 in Chicago, about 6,000 delegates representing 150 world religions gathered for a centennial celebration. In attendance were Buddhist, Orthodox, Anglican and other Protestant denominations, Catholic, Hindu, Confuscian, Native American, various Muslim groups, Taoist, the Fellowship of Isis, Covenant of the goddess, Wiccans, the Theosophical Society and many more. A smorgasbord of religion and a buffet of beliefs that showed the strong presence of goddess worshippers, witches and others of like mind. The document put together by those religions was called, *"Towards a Global Ethic, An Initial Declaration."*

This consists of a set of rules that all the religions of the world can agree upon. It replaces intolerant exclusionary teaching, such as those of the Bible, they say. Their belief includes secular humanism and it is a social contract for the New World Order. The purpose behind this is to provide an earth-based salvation for humanity, rather than salvation through Jesus, so they can build a millennial kingdom without Christ.

II Corinthians 11:14-15, "And no marvel; for Satan himself is transformed into an angel of light. Therefore it is no great thing if his ministers also be transformed as ministers of righteousness; whose end shall be according to their works." Some people preach another Jesus with another spirit and another gospel and there are other ministries that are inspired with this other spirit.

The true prophetic church of Jesus Christ will never be deceived and as long as it remains on this earth the power of God will prevail. In the book of Romans 8:29-39 it says: "For those God foreknew he also predestined to be conformed to the likeness of his Son, that he might be the firstborn among many brothers. And those he predestined, he also called; those he called, he also justified; those he justified, he also glorified. What, then, shall we say in response to this? If God is for us, who can be against us? He who did not spare his own Son, but gave him up for us all—how will he not also, along with him, graciously give us all things? Who will bring any charge against those whom God has chosen? It is God who justifies. Who is he that condemns? Christ Jesus, who died, more than that, who was raised to life, is at the right hand of God and is also interceding for us. Who shall separate us from the love of Christ? Shall trouble or hardship or persecution or famine or nakedness or danger or sword? As it is written: 'For your sake we face death all day long; we are considered as sheep to be slaughtered.' No, in all these things we are more than conquerors through him who loved us. For I am convinced that neither death nor life, neither angels nor demons, neither the present nor the future, nor any powers, neither height nor depth, nor anything else in all creation, will be able to separate us from the love of God that is in Christ Jesus our Lord."

Praise the Lord! We have Jesus interceding for us as individuals and for America as a nation birthed by divine providence. No power can remove His place of intercession and nothing can stop God from fulfilling his plans through the church of Jesus Christ. When I think about the church in America I am constantly reminded of the following verses in Ephesians 1:15-23 which says, "I have not stopped giving thanks for you, remembering you in my prayers. I keep asking that the God of our Lord Jesus Christ, the glorious Father, may give you the Spirit of wisdom and revelation, so that you may know him better, I pray also that the eyes of your heart may be enlightened in order that you may know the hope to which he has called you, the riches of his glorious inheritance in the saints, and his incomparably great power for us who believe. That power is like the working of his mighty strength, which he exerted in Christ when he raised him from the dead and seated him at his right hand in the heavenly realms, far above all rule and authority, power and dominion, and every title that can be given, not only in the present age but also in the one to come. And God placed all things under his feet and appointed him to be head over everything for the church, which is his body, the fullness of him who fills everything in every way."

As Paul wrote these words he knew God had a plan for future generations of the church. Every member of the church of Jesus Christ around the world today is included in the phrase "...not only in the present age, but also in the one to come." To declare that his body is irrelevant and powerless is a great mistake. We, the true church, are indwelt by the Holy Spirit who is so powerful, the antichrist cannot be revealed until this body of believers is taken out of the way by the supernatural act of God through the rapture. "Don't you remember that when I was with you I used to tell you these things? And now you know what is holding him back, so that he may be revealed at the proper time. For the secret power of lawlessness is already at work; but the one who now holds it back will continue to do so till he is taken out of the way" (II Thessalonians 2:5-7).

Yes, the spirit of antichrist is loose in the world. Yes, his plans are coming against America and they are for destruction, but he cannot have a victory here as long as there is one blood-bought, blood-sanctified believer standing in the gap. America is full of many that know the supernatural presence of God and we will not let prayer for America go until we see the absolute glory of the end-time harvest for which she was birthed. Yes, the spirit of antichrist is in the world, but even greater is the Spirit of the living God in the body of Christ, the church.

We are indwelt and surrounded by the answer for all the ages. We, the body of Christ, are the antidotes for the decadence of society in the world. Is the supernatural position and power of the church becoming clear to you? Is it becoming a firm reality?

Chapter Seven

Disintegrating Pillars
Not A Disintegrating Church

Traditionally, America is viewed as having four prophetic pillars. This very tradition has allowed America's true place in end-time prophecy to be overlooked. The four pillars are political, economical, military and religious. End-time prophecy study tends to view these four pillars as all-inclusive so the premise for America becomes one of no hope.

The economic pillar of prophecy in America is one we need to take a serious look at. Consumer debt is now at an alarming all time high doubling since 1990. American families owe 1.2 trillion dollars in debt not counting their mortgages. The lust for more consumer goods, high tech gadgets, luxury items, SUVs exotic vacations has caused people to "hock" their homes for equity loans. The mortgages of American homes are growing to alarming heights. When the family is destabilized and the home or basic shelter is threatened then the pillar of economy in America is showing a tremendous crack.

Despite the relative prosperity in the United States, there are some perturbing economic signs that continue to linger that are cause for concern among many experts. These are some of the factors that contribute to their concern and while any one of these factors is a cause for concern, cumulatively they create a cauldron of anxiety. Our nation's debt keeps growing because our dollar is high and not as many can afford to buy our products. Yet we have a glut of their products in the marketplace that can be imported at highly competitive prices. Credit card debt is at an all time high. Stocks are overpriced, we have contributed billions of dollars into communist countries and third world nations and most of these countries have no ability and no willingness to repay. The failure in the past of the savings and loans cost the taxpayer 1.3 trillion dollars. If you took $1,000 bills and stacked them, 1 million dollars would be 4 inches high. In comparison 1 trillion dollars would be 67 miles high.

Bankruptcies in America are at an all time high. Mergers and hostile takeovers are putting more money in the hands of fewer people. While all these things have been happening in America, a European economic colossus, a European superstate has been birthed and is now in the full bloom of manhood. Despite the failure of several attempts to form a European superstate in the past hinderances been overcome to create this plan of unity and power that exist today.

The Europeans now have formed a huge political, economic, military and amalgamation. They now have one foreign policy, a high court, political strength and control, economic control, one citizenship, one central bank, a common passport. Europe has become a profound economic influence on the West and it has also become the center of world religion. Europe is poised to assume dominance in the global economy and this has profound social, political and historical ramifications for the entire world.

This union is already the world's largest trading block, importing and exporting more than the USA and the Soviet Union combined. Its population is larger than America, and its gross domestic product is larger. At the same time there is an incredible disparity in the distribution of wealth and at this time many of the economies of the world are being severely shaken. China, Indonesia, Brazil, Mexico, Russia, Malaysia, Africa, Pakistan, Taiwan and most of the third world countries are in an economic downturn and some are on the edge of economic disaster.

To show the power that the European Union has achieved, an article with astonishing implication was seen in the July 4, 2001 Tulsa World Newspaper. It said, "EU blocks GE Honeywell Deal." Europe vetoed General Electric Company's $41 billion purchase of Honeywell International, Inc. The decision marked the first time a proposed merger between two U.S. companies were blocked solely by European regulators. The ruling was widely accepted after the companies failed to ease European fears that the deal would create an unfair dominant position in markets for jetliner engines and aircraft electronics.

This European intervention is a stunning indicator of the political and economic influence this body has worldwide, and the prophetic declaration of this European end-time confederation in Revelation 13, Daniel 7, and Revelation 17 is now a clear and present reality.

It is obvious that this economic pillar is being shaken, but at the same time the promise of God is clear and precise and full of hope for tomorrow. Consider Elijah at the brook Cherith that was in the process of drying up in the time of famine. He was fed by a raven and meat was brought to him morning and evening by a flesh-eating bird of voracious appetite. Thus God by a sovereign act reversed the laws of nature and commanded the raven to feed him, "There." Elijah, in the place of obedience was fed miraculously by God. The ensuing question is where did the raven get meat in the time of famine. Could it be that God directed this raven to Jezebel's table and there in the king's court, in the enemy's camp God transferred some resource from the possession of the unrighteousness to the hands of the righteous? When the child of God stays in the place of obedience, no matter how things seem to deteriorate externally, God will miraculously effect a transfer to your house. The enemy's camp is besieged by omnipotence and he cannot hold in bondage what God has declared is mine.

In times when economies are being shaken, rest assured that Jehovah Jireh will sovereignly intervene and divinely supply your need. As we see the pillar of the world's economy being shaken I am so thrilled that I belong to a body, the church, where it cannot be shaken (Hebrews 12:27,28) and that this is my testimony and my foundational belief.

The political pillar, is also an important component in the perceived four-fold foundation of prophecy? Because the problems we face are now global problems, the solutions that are demanded must be global in nature. The problems of environment, famine, societal chaos, military interventions, border conflicts, economic disorder, political tensions have all created a desperate need for a global coalition of nations to garnish enough influence and power so that from a position of a community of authorized nations, intractable problems can be dealt with.

No one can argue that if the world is united in its effort for peace, if it takes care of the environment and effectively opposes men of unbridled political ambition with no regard for the safety of his people, humanity will indeed enter a new phase of a New World hitherto unknown. The implication is that the international structure will be cast into a New World and nations will begin relating to one another in new ways. This political position is tenuous at best because many nations are governed by leaders with autocratic and dictatorial agendas and despite the fact that the desire of this political power-block of nations is to unite and polarize, there remain significant gaps and inconsistencies.

James 4:1,2 is a solemn reminder that it is the heart of man that is at the source of dispute and war and selfishness, and for a solution to be found it must deal with the heart of man. Revelation 17 is a clear picture that no political leader can gain control of people unless he possesses something that can transcend religious and social boundaries. There must be a syncretism of political acumen and religious belief. The antichrist, in the coming tribulation period will employ just such a tactic to use this ability of religion to bring humanity under his spell of control and domination. There is such an alliance taking place today as the alternate beliefs of Pantheism, astrology, a network of New Age doctrines, under the disguise of enlightenment, and cults of mysticism that challenge objective truth. This has been embraced by the political powers.

Monotheistic Pantheism which says, that all are one and all are God, has become a major tenet of this New Age duplicate, alternate faith. Man is born into this world both good and divine in his nature. They state that salvation depends on looking inward at one's spiritual nature and recognizing that the individual is god. This is precisely the reproduction of II Thessalonians 2:4,5 where the antichrist declares his godhood and is now creating that same spirit in the world today.

The plan is an age-old plan as found in Genesis 11. Both at Babel and today we find an effort to realize humanity's collective potential for greatness apart from the rule of the sovereign God. Satan has a specific objective until the world in a religious political system, which worships him and rejects Jerusalem. It is consequentially impossible to deal with the political pillar without seeing the inextricable knot between the religious and political pillars.

For the first time in history we have discovered that there is one planet with global ties. Now they speak of one human family and that we have to transcend all national, linguistic, cultural, social and religious differences. We have a chance to write a completely new history.

Based on the evidence of a single intelligence directing them, a common foundation has been laid. And mankind inadvertently is readying himself behind the system of the antichrist for a final assault on God's plan and God's people. There is a replay of the tower of Babel where, during its construction there was universal cooperation, global alliances, and transcended barriers. A global village in Genesis was created.

The political pillar involves the agendas of world leaders as they have desperately tried to find a mechanism, apart from God, so that problems of global magnitude can be solved. By virtue of their participation nations have to somehow cede some of their sovereign prerogatives, even some of their power to this governing planetary body.

The political pillar is also a prophetic pillar in prophecy. There is no country in the world with the freedoms found in America. America is the democracy of the world. The freedoms we take for granted, the rest of the world is dying for. As other governments fail, America is again being called upon for wisdom in the political arena. However, something very unusual is beginning to happen. America is yielding much of its decision-making power concerning world events to the United Nations. This too is part of the prophetic scenario.

In the end time, after the church is removed, the political power of the world will not rest in a democracy. It will be a dictatorship under the auspices of a man that the Bible calls the antichrist. The world is on the road to the New World Order and America is paving the way. If America supports this New World Order, it won't be hard to convince the world to do the same. America's acceptance in this arena is equivalent to the world's acceptance.

The political system of the world will soon be in the hands of the antichrist. It is imperative at this time, that the church reviews and comprehends its early history. America must also take a refresher course in her true background and inception, and not the rewritten version of the humanists.

It is clear that America will not be a strong political system in the last days. When all governments are usurped by antichrist, the greatest dictatorship the world has ever seen will be established. That cannot and will not happen until the saints of God are gone. Democracy is the gift of God to America and the concept of freedom came from the minds and hearts of men under the divine inspiration of the Holy Spirit. **It is imperative that people come to Christ now!**

Governments are falling every day. How much time is left only God knows. If we examine the dramatic role

America is playing in establishing the New World Order, our conclusion must be that the church of Jesus Christ is about to be removed! It is time to come to Jesus while you are still living in the greatest democracy in the world. I doubt very seriously that under the persecution of the antichrist, many will risk their lives and livelihood for the gospel's sake. I have seen hate in the eyes of men because I bear the name of Jesus. I have experienced government's failings, cities being burned, homes looted and children orphaned overnight by the horrors of war. Everything and everyone is expendable. There is no pity in the heart of a man trying to survive.

Man has a heart of sin and only the blood of Jesus can so change him that he can "love his enemy." I tell you now, many of you reading this book who do not know Jesus Christ as your Lord and Savior are capable of heinous actions. You do not believe you could kill someone but the truth is you are capable of anything when put to the test. Many soldiers live with the guilt and knowledge that what I am saying is true. Under antichrist and the, most demonic hate the world has ever known, I doubt that many will have the strength and fortitude to stand for Jesus. I implore you to come to Jesus now. I implore you to come while the Holy Spirit is moving and drawing men to Christ. Don't wait. Don't take the chance of being left behind. America and the rest of the world will literally experience a hell on earth once the church is gone. I was a miserable man and sinner before Jesus did a complete and wonderful work in me. He will do the same for you. Come just as you are. Come while there is still time.

The days are running out and soon that glorious event called the rapture (the disappearance of all Christians in the world) will happen. My prayer is that you will humble yourself, confess your sins and accept Jesus into your life. You have nothing to lose and everything to gain!

The military is another prophetic pillar that has played a role in keeping the world "safe for democracy." America is one of the most powerful nations in the world. Desert Storm proved to the world how technologically advanced this country really is. America has been the watchdog for the world. The world has found great security in America's military strength. America was instrumental in bringing about victory in World Wars I and II and her role in Desert Storm was more than apparent. The prophetic problem facing America is the antichrist will be in control of the military systems of the world. I find it interesting that leadership has sent American troops into Haiti, Somalia, the Middle East and other areas of the world. The unique thing here is our American troops are being sent over as a multi-international force. They are not going as Americans but as part of a larger one-world military concept. They do not wear the helmet of the American soldier but the blue beret of the United Nations!

We are closing military bases and reducing spending for our military budget. Why? The answer is simple; we are being prepared for the antichrist system. (I do not believe this switch will happen while the church is still in America.) God has always helped us in time of war. Some of our greatest leaders were military men who knew they needed the help of Almighty God. This report was given about George Washington:

"I heard a fine example today, namely, that His Excellency General Washington rode around among his army yesterday and admonished each and every one to fear God, to put the away wickedness that has set in and become so general, and to practice the Christian virtues. From all appearances, this gentleman does not belong to the so-called world of society, for he respects God's Word, believes in the atonement through Christ, and bears himself in humility and gentleness. Therefore, The Lord God has also singularly, yea, marvelously, preserved him from harm in the midst of countless perils, ambuscades, fatigues, etc., and has hitherto graciously held him in His hand as a chosen vessel." 3

Eddie Rickenbacker, the most celebrated American aviator in France during World War I, prayed:

"I pray to God every night of my life to be given the strength and power to continue my efforts to inspire in others the interest, the obligation and the responsibilities that we owe to this land for the sake of future generations—for my boys and girls—so that we can always look back when the candle of life burns low and say "Thank God I have contributed my best to the land that contributed so much to me." 4

We must realize that America is not a warmonger. At this point America is probably one of the most stable countries in the world. She has literally become the police force of the world. There is no changing the course of destiny for this New World Order. What is important is to realize that God has blessed America in times of war and has given her tremendous success where other nations have failed? The church is the foundation and channel for this blessing and will continue to be until the rapture.

The last prophetic pillar we need to look at is the pillar of religion. What was once the pillar of Christ in America has become the pillar of religion. Religiosity is desperately trying to replace Christianity and the result is a great deception that tries to pass itself off as the faith of America. It is extremely important for Christians to study and understand the history of America. It is only when we understand the early historical documents of this great country that we can perceive the place and position of Christ and Christianity as a fundamental founding principle of this nation. It always has been and it always will be founded on Christ as long as the church remains here!

The danger is New Age movement's ability to deceive many Americans as they lose touch with the true history of this nation. History has been rewritten to make the Christian covenants appear weak and old fashioned, or simply nonexistent. We must teach the historical truth in order to break the deceptive cycle of "all faiths welcome."

The prophetic purpose of the religious pillar is clear. It will be the denomination of the antichrist. It is hard to imagine the deception in the name of religion but the world saw a glimpse of it in Waco, Texas. One of the deadliest days in the history of America happened in the name of religion. These cults will increase in America and flow out in a false missionary zeal to the world. The Bible clearly states: "The Spirit clearly says that in the latter times some will abandon the faith and follow deceiving spirits and things taught by demons. Such teachings come through hypocritical liars, whose consciences have been seared as with a hot iron." 5

An alarming trend began happening in America during the sixties. Toward the end of the sixties, repeated shocks to the American psyche prepared the way for mesmerizing gurus. Coincidentally, changes in U.S. immigration laws allowed a number of Hindu, Buddhist and other spiritual masters to migrate here. Among them: the Maharishi

Mahesh Yogi, teacher of Transcendental Meditation, whose followers now run a fully accredited university in Fairfield, Iowa; Bhagwan Shree Rajneesh...who has since died, and the Rev. Sun Myung Moon, the South Korean whose well-heeled Unification Church is developing into a worldwide faith. Since these masters are their message, their movements are labeled by many as cults. 6

The deception is growing because America like the rest of the world is being prepared for the antichrist. There is hope though and not one person has to be deceived. The church is still the source of the truth and still holds the answers for the world. When one considers Jim Jones and the Jonestown massacre, Manson and his followers, David Koresh and the suicide/murder of numerous families, and understands that they are the precursors for antichrist, why would anyone want to follow "religion"?

Go back to your roots America, you will find belief in Jesus Christ as the very basic foundation on which this country was built. I have made my choice to follow Jesus, a man that never killed anyone but gave His life for mine.

There are two systems in the world. These two systems are polarized and will never meet. One is energized by the spirit of the antichrist; the other is infused with the life of Jesus, in the world but not of the world. Which are you a part of? I belong to the body of Christ, the church. Its destiny is to overcome so it is still the most powerful and prophetic body in the world today.

Chapter Eight

Back To Basics

A nation's youth is its future and to direct that future to a desired end one has only to control its collective mind. Hitler knew this principal well. In an address on May 1, 1937, Hitler expounded, "This new Reich will give its youth to no one, but will itself take youth and give to youth its own education and its own upbringing." [1.]

A very early example of this strategy occurs in the first chapter of Daniel: "Then the king ordered Ashpenaz, chief of his court officials, to bring in some of the Israelites from the royal family and the nobility—young men without any physical defect, handsome, showing aptitude for every kind of learning, well informed, quick to understand, and qualified to serve in the king's palace. He was to teach them the language and literature of the Babylonians.... They were to be trained for three years, and after that they were to enter the king's service" (Daniel 1:3-4, 5b).

Both leaders knew the value of capturing and manipulating the minds of their youth through targeted and focused education. Whatever end product was desired, a precise plan of education ensured that the next generation to come to power would rule according to the established plan.

In establishing the colony in New England to exemplify God's greatest and highest good, the "city upon a hill,"[3] the Puritans saw the need for a system of education as one of their first and foremost priorities. This educational system was based entirely upon the Holy Scriptures. Regardless of the school's form, home-based or institutional, the Bible formed curriculum's core. The oldest existing copy of the New England Primer demonstrates the Puritan's use of religious rhymes to teach the alphabet.

The most widely known, Bible-based teaching tool of America's early schools was McGuffey's Reader. Produced by William Holmes McGuffey, it was the mainstay of public education until 1920. It was one of the most widely used and influential textbooks of all time. One hundred and twenty-five million copies had been sold by 1963, and countless American children learned to read and write from it. McGuffey insisted that the Bible was the only source of true education. He firmly believed Christianity was the foundation of all American liberties, and he considered the Ten Commandments and the teachings of Jesus essential to a quality education. This attitude pervaded all levels of education.

In establishing Harvard, Yale and Columbia the gospel was foundational. It became the basis of instruction for future leaders of America. Harvard's School of Divinity played an exceptionally pivotal role, as the ministers it produced became the educators of the early school system. The founders of these early colleges believed learning apart from Christ was vain and useless. These divinity graduates had one purpose, to pass on the Christian legacy to the next generation. It is an important fact that out of the first 108 schools established in America, 106 were opened and operated by the Christian church. America's early educational system was wholly Christian. We see in its birth, its policies even its textbooks the gospel of Christ was its driving force.

In contrast, today's education has strayed far from its Puritan roots. Based on humanism and self-reliance, we have seen a tremendous slide in character and academics. Prayer has been replaced with transcendental meditation and new age spiritism; brotherly love with homosexuality; pure lives with teenage pregnancy and drug abuse; abstinence with promiscuity, the threat of venereal diseases and aids. The third largest reason for the death of a minor is now murder. We must return to the God-given principles that created this great country. The media would have us believe that all hope is lost. The truth is the church needs to awaken to the knowledge of the history of America and apply the oil of healing to a wounded generation. The church must once again set the standard. We need Christian teachers to go into the public school system and take a stand; to pick up the instruction of its youth where the public systems have failed. Jesus was very clear when he said: "And whoever welcomes a little child like this in my name welcomes me. But if anyone causes one of these little ones who believe in me to sin, it would be better for him to have a large millstone hung around his neck and to be drowned in the depths of the sea" (Matthew 18:6).

We have to value this generation and realize the same power that created men and women such as George Washington, John Adams Abraham Lincoln, Betsy Ross and George Washington Carver still exists in committed believers of the Lord Jesus Christ. He cannot fail. He still has the power to transform a life.

America's youth needs to hear this not only from the pulpit on Sundays but through their educators during the week. The Bible and its principles for living must be brought back into education. If the public schools refuse this assignment, then the church must pick it up.

Ministers and teachers of the gospel need to equip themselves not only with the fundamentals of the Bible, but with a knowledge of the historical Christian heritage of America. It is imperative that the old calling of minister as educator be reinstituted to reclaim the minds of our youth.

We have read about the major problems of the schools in the fifties-kids chewing gum in class, throwing paper, not staying in line, and pushing another classmate. What happened to turn our precious educational system into almost a prison-like atmosphere with metal detectors, security gates, lock-down procedures, extra armed security and special lock up rooms to hold the drugs, alcohol, and firearms brought to school daily and confiscated daily.

What happened to that hug and kiss goodbye to our children and the security we felt sending them down the street to the public school system? The smile became a cry when children were forced to watch their classmates die in front of their eyes and the hug becomes an embrace of fear because they have had to run for their lives.

The answer is simple, prayer is gone out of the public school system and the standards that our original schools upheld are now rejected because they include the teaching of the Bible and the compassion of Jesus Christ.

The generation that went to school and missed the education based on morality and honesty has become the generation that has a 700% divorce rate. It is the generation where millions of girls a year get pregnant out of wedlock. It is the generation that substitutes drugs and alcohol for prayer and Bible study. It is the generation that has the highest suicide rate among its teens. It is the generation that seems destined to accept the deceptions of the New World Order because they do not know the history of America and how the gospel made this one of the greatest nations on the face of the earth and how millions left all they had, to endure hardships just to come and kiss the soil of America and call her their home. They are a generation who doesn't understand the value of life, over one million abortions a year, children killing children in the schools and now children are becoming murderers at an alarming rate and being institutionalized for life.

The greatness of America does not lie in humanism, new age, or environmentalism. The greatness of America is and always will be found in the church of Jesus Christ, built out of love and compassion for one another and considering all men equal and brothers. Education apart from the gospel is why we have the X generation.

We must bring back the original standard of teaching that made this country one of the most prosperous in the world. Church teaching should be one of the highest professions a person can be called into. Only if we lay our lives down for our brothers will we truly effect national and spiritual change in our nation.

Chapter Nine

"Remain In Him"

The government in America is made up of three parts: legislative, judiciary and executive. The legislative branch makes the law, the judiciary interprets the law, and the executive executes the law. It is a pattern straight from the Bible; God makes the law, Jesus interprets the law, and the Spirit residing in the church executes the law. That means whatever God does on the face of the earth in this dispensation he is going to do through the church. Do you have any idea what that means? That means when God gets ready to do something, the United Nations doesn't matter, the Pentagon doesn't matter, Russia doesn't matter, the Gentiles don't matter, and the Rights movements don't matter. When God gets ready to move, He will do it through His church. No wonder the enemy has attacked the church, the church is the executive of God.

Satan experienced firsthand the power and glory of a baby church, and he couldn't destroy it. Now that the church is 2,000 years old its muscles have gotten bigger, it has gotten larger, there are more prayer warriors, more preachers, more teachers and more believers than at any other time in its history. He is powerless against it.

To understand the glorious destiny of the church there must be a clear understanding of the origin of the church. Genesis 2:22,23 gives a profound revelation that is filled with New Testament theology. God created Adam and saw that Adam needed a helpmeet, so he placed Adam under divine anasthetic, put him to sleep and took a rib from him. From that rib, God made Eve and she became bone of his bone and flesh of his flesh. Her identity, her purpose and future, her life were all decided by the nature of Adam that was placed in her when God formed her from Adam's rib.

I Corinthians 15:45 calls Jesus the last Adam, by calling him the last Adam, God connects Him to the first Adam. By virtue of this connection we can deduce that the last Adam would need an "Eve," just like the first Adam.

On the cross of Calvary, the soldier pierced the side of Jesus and the symbolism resonates as on the Day of Pentecost God created an "Eve" or a helpmeet for His son. Thus Ephesians 5:30 becomes a reality, we are bone of His bone and flesh of His flesh. This is the identical scripture that is quoted in Genesis 2:23.

Just as Eve's destiny, purpose and life were decided by her connection with Adam, so too the church's very existence is contingent on its connection with the last Adam who has given His identity, His life, His purpose to the body of Christ. This is the origin of the Church and because of this, the power, indestructibility, and glory of the church are seen. We are like the burning bush that never burns out. Just as Jonah in the belly of the fish was swallowed but not digested, the church will never be masticated by the enemy. The resurrection life of Jesus is a part of that identity and it is infused into the lives of those that He has touched. What a joy to know that sin and death have no power to prevail against this resurrected church. It may assault, but never prevail.

There is no excuse for the church in America not to be the most potent example of God's power on the face of the earth. We live in a free society. We can go to church, praise, worship and meet together anytime and anyplace we want. There are no soldiers crashing the church doors down and hauling the believers off to jail. There are no machine guns opening fire on the faithful. There are no boarded up and confiscated churches. Pastors are not being killed and made examples of, to terrify their congregations. There is no excuse for the church in America to be so apathetic. Millions around the world have had their blood spilled to gain one second of the freedom we enjoy. We are a free church! We must rise up now and take back the souls of men for the King is coming.

We are not a poor church. In fact, we are one of the wealthiest groups of people in the world today. If it takes money to move the machinery of the gospel. Then America has been truly blessed. The technology to present the gospel around the world comes out of America. The greatest Christian broadcasting networks have been birthed here. Church, it is a blessing and gift from Almighty God to reach lost men, women and children in these last days.

Why would God create and give such a gift to mankind only to destroy it before the church is removed?

The end-time message of Christ is going around the globe due to American technology. It's the very ingenious, miraculous tool he has given to the American church. The end-time message of Christ is going around the globe from the base of America!

America's prophetic place in God's plan coupled with its blessed financial capabilities paved the way. This system is not in the hands of a New Age spirit. This system is not under the control of a dictatorial government. This system is not for an elite few and the masses be damned. No, this system is in the hands of the most powerful group of people the world has ever seen. It is in the hands of the church and we had better not fumble the ball.

The church in America is stronger than any military army in the world. Paul made it clear: "I beg you that when I come I may not have to be as bold as I expect to be toward some people who think that we live by the standards of this world. For though we live in the world, we do not wage war as the world does. The weapons we fight with are not the weapons of the world. On the contrary, they have divine power to demolish strongholds. We demolish arguments and every pretension that sets itself up against the knowledge of God, and we take captive every thought to make it obedient to Christ" (II Corinthians 10:4,5).

Church, our power is not found in tanks, missiles, armies, or nuclear weapons. Our power comes from a source so profound that it is activated and ready for use every time we fall on our knees and cry out to God. There is not a nation, government, people or religion that has access to that miraculous, supernatural, unearthly power.

Church, that power is yours and it has been so in America for over 225 years. Nothing has happened to take away that power, but the false witness of the media, tries to convince you otherwise. With their words they try to convince you that you have lost your momentum as a people of God. Satan is a liar. In the book of 1 John 2:20-27 we are reminded: "But you have an anointing from the Holy One, and all of you know the truth. I do not write to you because you do not know the truth, but because you do know it and because no lie comes from the truth. Who is the liar? It is the man who denies that Jesus is the Christ. Such a man is the antichrist—he denies the Father and the Son. No one who denies the Son has the Father; whoever acknowledges the Son has the Father also. See that what you have heard from the beginning remains in you. If it does, you also will remain in the Son and in the Father. And this is what he promised us—even eternal life. I am writing these things to you about those who are trying to lead you astray. As for you, the anointing you received from him remains in you, and you do not need anyone to teach you. But as his anointing teaches you about all things and as that anointing is real, not counterfeit—just as it has taught you, remain in him."

Remain in him! That is the trumpet's message, which I have put to my mouth with the writing of this book.

Resurrection power resides in true uncompromised believers of America. The doors to our sanctuaries have been closed by none other than ourselves. It is startling and unsettling that churches all across America have relegated themselves to a Sunday morning service only! We wilfully close the doors on Sunday night because we are afraid our people won't come out. This is a shame and should not be so. You aren't preaching so your people can enjoy an evening out. You have been called to so sear the consciences of men that profound change will take place in their lives and families.

It is a reproach to us that we have wilfully closed the churches during the week and settled for a once a week dose of light conviction. There are enough unsaved people, drug-addicted children, broken families and lives in America that if the doors were open every night and we as the church got busy in prayer and evangelism, we could not contain the harvest that would come in. I beg you in the name of Jesus Christ our Lord, "Remain in him!"

Chapter Ten

Prophecy Belongs
To
The Church

The most poignant statement that I can make to you as a man of God is, "the world is not going to get better." I'm not a politician, I'm not an economist nor am I an expert in military or ecology matters. One thing I am is a servant of the living God and I have read the book and I can tell you how it all ends. In the book of Matthew 24:3-6;42-46, the point is made: "As Jesus was sitting on the Mount of Olives, the disciples came to him privately. 'Tell us,' they said 'when will this happen, and what will be the sign of you coming and the end of the age?' Jesus answered: 'Watch out that no one deceives you. For many will come in my name, claiming, I an the Christ, and will deceive many. You will hear of wars and rumors of wars, but see to it that you are not alarmed. Such things must happen, but the end is still to come.... Therefore keep watch, because you do not know on what day your Lord will come. But understand this: If the owner of the house had known at what time of night the thief was coming, he would have kept watch and would not have let his house be broken into. So you also must be ready, because the son of Man will come at an hour when you do not expect him. Who then is the faithful and wise servant, whom the master has put in charge of the servants in his household to give them their food at the proper time? It will be good for that servant whose master finds him doing so when he returns.' "

Prophecy is the revelation of God given to the church first. It is our compass to guide us and keep us going in the right direction. The world is basically the stage upon which prophecy is being enacted. The church must stay attuned to current events and we must be in tune in America to our history. Our past can secure the future if we are aware of the truth that the past contains. I admonish every preacher of the gospel of Jesus Christ in America to go back and get the foundational truths of this country firmly renewed in his mind. Our forefathers were great people of character and even I as an immigrant to this country, am blessed and inspired by the commitment and sacrifices the early church leaders made for this great land. *America's God and Country Encyclopedia of Quotations* is a tremendous book tracing the great Christian history of this nation. I believe that when you sit down and read the written prayers of George Washington you will be so inspired by the Holy Spirit that prayer will take on a powerful new meaning in your life.

We must, as preachers of the gospel be the servants who are doing what Jesus asked, preach the truth of Jesus Christ. America, you are at a glorious and dangerous crossroads. You can continue to believe the lies or you can shake the dust off the greatest book ever written, the Bible and stand up and be counted as worthy by the blood of the Lamb. In the very near future the eastern sky is going to be split and Jesus shall appear. He will rapture the church out of the world and so forever more we will be with him. You are facing the end. New age, New World order will try to convince you that they can make the world a safe and sane place. They will try to convince you that they can clean up the planet earth and everything will be alright. Don't believe the lie. Prophecy tells us very clearly that this earth will pass away. This belief that we can change the world apart from the supernatural power of God is the system of antichrist.

Church, we are not called to save the planet, the seas, the whales, the spotted owl, rivers, mountains, valleys, or air quality. We as the church of Jesus Christ are called to preach the gospel with such truth, conviction, and simplicity, that we interrupt the destinies of men who are on their way to hell. A man's destination can be changed from hell to heaven if we are wise and faithful servants putting food on the table that will satisfy the hunger and quench the thirst of lost and hurting souls. We are also to stand with our brothers in Israel and pray for the peace of Jerusalem. We are one with Israel, America, and if we ever lose sight of that truth, we will be held to the specific judgments of scripture reserved for the nations that turn on Israel. God is not a liar. He means what He has written and he will do what He says.

Church in America this your assignment from God. America this is your prophetic role in these last days. We are not puppets on the string of the atheistic media. We are not in a sleep unto death but I pray by the power of the Holy Spirit you will be forever changed by the reading of this book. For every person who chooses to live holy and for every person who says no to the devil the enemy loses ground. When you say no to hell and refuse to be the garbage dump for his refuse of lies you become a light shining out in darkness. When things look dark, it is always reassuring to turn in the direction of light and let the illumination guide.

For every person who will say I am a child of the living God and my body is the house for his Holy Spirit, and keep that house spotless, the devil has lost you as a candidate for hell. The devil will never control what he doesn't own-the people who still love Jesus, praise him and magnify his name! I cannot over emphasize to you church your part in this country, to stand in the word of God. Don't sell your soul to the people who are merchandising the gospel of Jesus. Don't sell your soul for one more ounce of so-called pleasure. Don't sell your soul to the humanistic secular mindset. You have the power as one individual or millions in this country, to interrupt the cycle of sin and let the saving grace of Jesus Christ change lives.

The church in America is about to awaken to its finest hour. America fights a battle that cannot be won at the ballot box. Her need is not the need for a new morality but a need to have morals based on the word of God. This is the power of the American church today. As God has graciously allowed me to travel around the world, I have noticed a stirring in America. Mediocrity is being replaced with a spirit of excellence in the church. People who were on the sidelines for years because of compromise, arrogance and self-sufficient attitudes are now being set on fire by the power of the Holy Spirit. This is happening in hundreds of churches in America. It is beginning to have a rippling effect which will be an earthquake to the world.

God is turning the tide. "America is to young to die," said Leonard Ravenhill, one of the great preachers gone by. This is a day when permissiveness is the unwritten law of millions, but pure words from impassioned preachers anointed by the power of the Holy Spirit can change that. A call for revival within the church of America should be trumpeted from one end of America to another. Yes, America can die but it would have to be by suicide, it would only be because she thinks that God is dead.

I am hear to tell you that the God of America is not dead! The God of America is still on His throne. The God in America is still blessing and changing the lives of its citizens. The God of America is still producing the greatest evangelistic teams from the scripture of Matthew 28:19 "Go ye therefore, and teach all nations, baptizing them in the name of the Father, and of the Son, and of the Holy Ghost:"

America you need to remember from whence you came and go back to the inspired sermons of great men of God like Billy Graham who preaches with such simplicity;

"Jesus Christ can come into your life, sweep it clean and give you a new power to follow his ways. You will never find total satisfaction until Christ lives in your heart." You're going out into eternity. Jesus has his hand outstretched to you. He wants to lead you into heaven.

"I'm asking you to receive Christ in a new way, to say 'You are my savior and Lord and Master, and I am going to put you first.

"Many of us are so comfortable in our world that is controlled by the devil that we don't want to go to heaven. Many of you promote your own spiritual death.

"You attend church, you are respected in your community, but you are a fraud. You need to come to the cross and let Christ change you and give you the power to live the Christian life.

"Jesus is asking you to surrender all. Will you invite Jesus in? He wants to change your life. God will totally forgive you because of Christ.

"You say, 'I believe in Christ.' Do you believe enough to put your life into his hands?" 1

Jimmy Carter the 39th president of the United States said this about Billy Graham: "There is no way anyone can describe the impact that Billy Graham has had on our city, our state, our nation and the world. Of all who bring the message of peace from the Prince of Peace, Billy Graham is at the forefront." God raised up this great evangelist to save the world through the message of Jesus Christ. He has raised up you and me for the same purpose. He is not a respecter of persons. Those same words coming from your mouth inspired and backed by the Holy Spirit will have the same effect on a soul-conversion.

The church in America contains the glory of the living God. My Father is a loving Father and I do not believe for one second that he will destroy me because of the sins of the antichrist system. Church you are not deaf, dumb, blind or dead! You are the only living thing in this world that keeps growing and growing and growing. America, you are a tree of righteousness, if you can hear what the Spirit is saying. I, as a lost soul came under your magnificent shade and was refreshed by the renewing of my mind.

America, God is still shedding his grace on thee.

Chapter Eleven

Jerusalem On The Rise
And
The World In Demise

You need to ask yourself an important question. Whom do I serve? A large percentage of the church in America is not really committed to Christ but attends services because of the charismatic personality behind the pulpit. These people are submitted and connected to the church organization. There is a tremendous difference between this group and the true church, which is connected and committed to Christ and establishes that fact by its members supporting a local church. They are the true worshippers of God. They do not belong to the "I follow Paul" or "I follow Apollos" group. People have so many needs and they will only be met when they find the help they need in submitted and surrendered vessels to Jesus Christ.

Many churches today are being built on the personality of its leadership. This is a very sensitive area and one that needs constant prayer. With the advent of television and its great sphere of influence, it is understandable how gospel stars are born. What is important is to stay focused on Jesus Christ especially as things around us deteriorate.

It is true that things are not getting better in the world. The world is falling apart, and things are going from bad to worse, but in the church things are getting better. In the world you have doom and gloom but in the church it is power and boom. The point to remember although all these negative assertions are correct-things are bad, the world does seem crazy, economies are failing, governments are crumbling but they all point to a greater event about to happen, the rapture of the church!

The one we are looking for is about to break through the sky and we had better have our eyes open waiting to behold him and not the latest personality. Until that time we are left with two choices. We can get angry and depressed as the world continues on its course of decay and deterioration and give into the antichrist system, or we can come to the house of God with our hands in the air to praise and magnify the name of Jesus. We can acknowledge that, Lord willing, we are going to be alive when this great event happens. Until then, we are going to give life our best shot. Firmly fix it in your mind that you will serve Him, you will praise Him, you will magnify His name. The choice is really yours.

One of the most electrifying prophecies in the Bible is, Luke 21:24-28. "Jerusalem will be trampled on by the Gentiles until the times of the Gentiles are fulfilled." This is an exciting scripture because we are the generation that has seen Jerusalem turned back into the hands of the Jewish nation. Now that this prophecy has begun to come to pass we can look for four prophetic signs to be fulfilled.

1.   The Gentile world will begin the process of deterioration.
2. There will be signs in the sun, moon, and stars.
3. Men's hearts will fail for fear.
After you see these three the fourth will happen.
4. Jesus will come in the clouds with great power and glory.

We will deal with the sign number one in a little more detail. Isn't it interesting that God did not pick LA,

London, Moscow, Perth, Hong Kong or any other city to be " the city of God"? God sovereignly chose the city of Jerusalem and declared that this city would hold the key of several end-time prophecies. For two thousand five hundred and fifty-three years Jerusalem was controlled by the Gentiles. She was attacked over forty-eight times and destroyed twice. Now in the last days God says Jerusalem will become the focal point of the world; it doesn't matter what governments say, armies do or countries believe. God said Jerusalem's state would be the sign to believers the clock is ticking for the return of Christ.

Something amazing happened in June of 1967, we now call it the six-day war. One thing we need to understand in scripture is the church is spiritual Israel; the nation is physical Israel. Physical Israel has a physical temple which is to be built to house the glory of God; spiritual Israel has the glory of God housed in each believer, whose body is the temple of the Lord. Physical Israel has a physical destiny on the earth; spiritual Israel has a destiny in heaven. Physical Israel is under Abraham's covenant; spiritual Israel is under the new covenant. What God does in physical Israel will be manifested in some fashion in spiritual Israel. If you want to know what God is going to do in the church, look at Israel.

In June 1967, God in typological and prophetic reflection erected a marker. Jordan, Syria and Egypt invaded Israel to take away her land and give her no place to dwell. God miraculously turned the invasion around. Instead of capturing the land, Israel chased the invaders out and claimed new land for herself. From Jordan, Israel won East Jerusalem past the Jordan river; from Syria, Israel won the Golan Heights; from Egypt, Israel won the Sinai. The enemy invaded to steal from God's people but, by the power of the covenant of God, he turned it around; instead of a taking away from Israel there was an increase in her borders!

Praise God because even though the enemy has come in to rob, kill, and destroy God is about to move through spiritual Israel, the church, and increase her borders! The harvest is coming in. The enemy has used false religion, the New Age movement, psychic phenomena and false messiahs to take spiritual land, but in the name of Jesus through the power found in the church, we will take back the stolen sheep. We will bring them back to the fold from which they have strayed. We will not be looking to a charismatic leader to begin this work. This work will begin when the truth of who you are in Christ is settled within you. It is the blessing of every believer.

Like Jerusalem after 2,000 years in the enemies' hands, the church is about to shake off the trials and tribulations Satan has tried to destroy it with, and stand in a prophetic place of divine placement by God. Jerusalem is no longer in the hands of the Gentiles. From that day in 1967 and continuing even now, we are watching the Gentile world crack and break apart. The boasting, the arrogance, the wealth, power and authority of the Gentile world is decaying and dying. Church, when you realize your ministry and work are not based on the dollar, but on the faith of God, finances will never stop you again. I know a God who can multiply your dollar. I know a God who can multiply your finances, groceries, gas or income. I know a God who has the power to supersede the dollar and the economy. Church, your life is not governed by the power of the economy, that system will fail. Jesus is the source of our hope and future.

In 1971 America came off the gold standard. In 1973 oil embargoes began to happen, and gas went from fifty cents a gallon to one dollar a gallon overnight. We were forced to have even and odd days for gas rationing. In the government, presidential calamities continued. President Nixon was forced to resign from office, and assassination attempts have been made on almost every president since the '60s. America finally pulled out of Vietnam with tremendous, negative public opinion bearing down on the brave men and women who fought there and gave their lives. Those returning were never given the "welcome home" other veterans received, and to this day feel the betrayal of their country in their hearts.

The banking system began to collapse with the great savings and loans scandals. Iran and Iraq went to war with each other and over one million people were killed. Homosexuality came out of the closet and became a major contributor to moral decline. Pornography flooded the global markets and is now totally uncensored on the global computer system of the Internet. The moral erosion of the youth in the sixties has now brought the heartbreak of venereal diseases and the plague of Aids like the world has never known before. Church, the Gentile world is disintegrating exactly as the scripture said it would.

Church, we are the only hope for the world today. The only time left is being given by the divine time clock of Almighty God. We must get busy. God is "not willing that any should perish." Church, the media has done a tremendous job of getting your hope from heaven to earth. I hope I can get a better job. I hope I can make more money. I hope I can buy a bigger car. I hope I can get a bigger home. I hope the economy does better. I hope the government does something to stop crime. If the enemy

can get your hope tied up with the world through deceit
and fraud then you have lost the battle.

Church, our hope is not in the things of this world, but
in the living Christ. If we get caught in the devil's lie,
hope in the world's goods and system, then we lose the
battle of faith! Faith becomes a catchword or an illusion
such as, God forbid, I hope someday I have faith to
believe for faith. Shout "no" to hope in the system of this
world.

The only viable solution for this last day's church is
faith, dependency, commitment and hope in Christ. Christ
and the hope we have in him are the only things that can
change and maintain a life in this present hour. The
economy, the government, the crime, they will not get
better. The new-agers and one-worlders will not
accomplish peace on earth. Only the Holy Spirit moving
in the midst of his body, the church, can cause peace to
increase on this earth. God will provide better houses,
cars, and the other material things you need to help you
get the gospel message out and win souls for his kingdom.
Heaven help you if you lose your perspective and depend
on the substance and not the creator. Church, our
perspective must change. Our hope is in **the day when
Christ comes to take us away! Church, this is your
hope and nothing less.**

Yes, the Gentile world is cracking but I am a child of
the living God. I am a Christian and although I live in the
Gentile world I am not part of it. I am a Christian and
subject to the authority and resurrected power of God. I
am a new man, a new creature in Christ Jesus. If you are
saved you are neither Jew nor Gentile, you are a new man;
you make up the body of Christ and you are called, "the

church." That means the cracking of the Gentile system needn't break you!

How then should you respond to the doom and gloom since it is a reality. You must realize that joining the body of Christ is the smartest thing to do. You're not being spiritual when you join a good local church, you're being smart. The Gentile world is moving at record speed into the antichrist system and the only escape out of it is into Christ's body, the church. Sin is a hard taskmaster and demands worship and surrender. How can a man say "yes" to sin— premarital sex, adultery, disease, and the possibility of death—and "no" to God? Sin will deaden your mind and you will believe the lie.

If you are saved, you have a lot to rejoice in and be grateful for. You are out of the Gentile system and belong to the body of Christ, and God is moving through His body with great power. Everyday we hear of banks closing, governments failing, wars beginning, and successful businesses suddenly going bankrupt. But, you never hear of the disintegration of churches that are founded on Bible principles, preaching Biblicial doctrines, living in Biblical light. These churches are sending Bibles to Russia and other foreign fields in record numbers. These churches are sending missionaries out, and going on television to transmit the Gospel to millions of homes simultaneously. The world is hearing in an instant what took centuries before. These churches are touching the world. These men and women of God are born again and not subject to the Gentile breaking. Yes, you will see the disintegration of the world, but you will experience the supernatural power of God bringing in the final man before He splits the sky and takes us home!

It is so important to stay focused on Jesus and not charismatic leadership, to keep setting the standard of righteousness so when the sinner has had his fill of grief, he can turn to you, his neighbor, for hope and you can introduce him to the "hope" of all ages. The church will be the only standard to come back to for a sick and depraved society. Only the church will have the power to deliver men, women, and children from lives of demonized living. Only the church will continue to grow and become powerful because it is the last hope for a world that is quickly on its way to antichrist. Only the church full of the miraculous power of Jesus Christ can draw dying men and restore lives.

America, the greatest organization in your country is not your zillion dollar corporation, your capitalism, your public school system, nor your charities, your greatest organization is the church of Jesus Christ. God has blessed America because of the church. He will not destroy the very instrument he created while there is still so much to do, and it can only be done through you, the church.

We are the church, the crucible of God's power to the world. We hold his power, greatness, love, and forgiveness. The church is still being added to daily by the power of the Holy Spirit touching men's lives with the knowledge of Jesus Christ. America, you are standing at the door of revival: Revelation 3:7-11 states, ". . .These are the words of him who is holy and true, who holds the key of David. What he opens no one can shut, and what he shuts no one can open. I know your deeds. See, I have placed before you an open door that no one can shut. I know that you have little strength, yet you have kept my word and have not denied my name....Since you have kept my command to endure patiently, I will also keep you from the hour of trial that is going to come upon the whole world to test those who live on the earth. I am coming soon. Hold on to what you have, so that no one will take your crown."

Church, the door is open, run through and rescue men's souls from the darkest hour the world will ever know.

Chapter Twelve

The Conclusion:

It is time to get up out of our complacent beds of compromise and take a stand. It is time to stop allowing the secular media to preach from the altars of fraud. It is time to think clearly and speak honestly. It is time to restore the truth about America's history of Christianity, which is at the core of her major documents, state constitutions and oaths. It is time to acknowledge that every president since Washington (except one) has taken the oath of office with his hand on the Bible. It is time to expect holiness and righteousness from our Christian leaders first and from our governmental leadership second. It is time to speak out to the teachers, counselors, principals, and administrators of the public school system and demand to be heard. Morality must be the standard taught to our youth. It is time to renew commitments to one another, our families, wives, husbands, and children, to become so cohesive that the world cannot tear us apart. It is time to rise up and be the church to this lost and dying world. It is time to stop thinking of religion as a private matter. If our forefathers believed that lie we would not be sitting in a free America.

The Bible sells more than any other book in the world, and Americans publish and print more Bibles than any other country. The American church is responsible for the translation of the Bible into every major foreign language in the world. A book of such magnitude should be taught in our school system. It is rarely studied and not often presented even as a work of literature. It would be hard to find an American home that did not have at least one Bible in it. We must become readers of this great gift to mankind and wipe out Biblical illiteracy. A lack of knowledge produces severe consequences. It is time for blood-bought Christians to take out the Bible and consume its pages. America's moral vacuum exists because she has ignored the greatest book on the face of the earth. Not only have we ignored it but also we are ignorant of its contents. Out of such ignorance we have allowed the world to interpret it for us. That is a calamity and a shame.

When America rejected the Bible from its school curriculum, she gave up the unity that made this country great. Christianity was the common ground this country was built on. Church, stand up and be counted. The enemy has come in to tell you that Bibles are no longer allowed in the public school system, but the Koran; writings of Buddha; and New Age, witchcraft, and transcendental meditation literature are the replacements to choose from. Church, the God that America prays to, trusts in, and surrenders allegiance to, is the God of Christianity and the public schools of America. We have the Ten Commandments on the Supreme Court walls not the teachings of secular humanists. Our money says, "In God we trust," not the number of the psychic hotline.

Church, are you getting the vision? Are you beginning to see you must get vocal? Time is short and the church is about to be removed from the face of the earth. It is time to be bold and speak out in the name of Jesus.

Pastors, if America is ever going to regain her greatness, it must begin with you. You must begin to preach with conviction, simplicity, and expectation. Man must be told he is a sinner. Jesus is the only answer for the redemption of this world. The rebirth of America will come through the gospel of Jesus Christ.

Pastors, you hold the key that will open the door to change. You have been given more authority to change things than the president of the United States has. You are the called and anointed vessels God wants to use in this hour.

Pastors, you are the instrument in the hand of a divine craftsman. You belong to a generation that is motivated by how well something is communicated to them. This generation is waiting for your voice to communicate the salvation message with power. Are you ready to become holy incendiaries spreading the fire of revival every time you get in the pulpit? Your words should be like fire, burning away the dross of compromised apathetic lives.

As Isaiah had a burning coal touch his mouth, are you ready for that same fire from the altar of God? The only way this kind of anointing will flow from you is if you allow compromise, selfishness, and control to be purged from your character. You need to settle a question in your mind. Can you serve God apart from the gain of mammon? You cannot serve both. You must give up one or the other. When you make that fundamental decision, you will never again be reserved or cautious about what you say. You will look at your congregation through the eyes of a true shepherd and have a boldness to ignite holiness within their lives and homes. You will have a new freedom to witness in the power of the Holy Spirit, as did the apostles of the early church.

Expect something to happen in your churches with this type of preaching. Hearts will melt, and worship will come forth. The lost will come to God and revival will break out all around you. True preaching is revelation of a truth, which you already know, in a greater measure. This allows for miracles to take place. When the listener begins to hear the revealed truth, his/her life will change forever.

Pastor, you must be inspired first in order to inspire your sheep. It is time to get before God. It is time to lock yourself in a closet of prayer and come out only after a live coal has seared your heart, soul, body, mind and spirit. It is when you feel this cleansing and anointing that God can speak to you prophetically. People tend to resist change but when they see the change in you and hear the revealed truth, they will surrender to the living God or leave to join the compromised, antichrist religious system of the world.

No one can sit still-movement, one way or the other, will happen. It will take more courage than you have ever had before to speak for God in these last days. Those who have one foot in church and one foot out, want to hear smooth words. Settle it in your heart now! You do not need the security man can give you. The security you need can only come from God. As the prophetic message of fire comes from your mouth it should be like thunder in the ears of the hearer. I pray God will give you that courage to stand up and be counted. As Paul prayed for boldness, I implore you to ask for the same and more. Idealistic words will never change a man. Lofty ideas will never build the kingdom of God. Hollow words will never have substance, but with only continue to expand the moral vacuum of society. Truth, courage, fire and simplicity are the key words you need to place in your being. Only an inspired word from the Holy Spirit will sear a conscience, burn away dross and refine for purity.

Every service should find you awed by the anticipation of what God is about to do through you. Every service is crucial. Every need is different and you cannot meet the needs, only Christ can through your surrendered life and message of the gospel. If a man walks out of your service untouched by Jesus Christ, it will be a shame. People must have their ears opened. It is only with divinely inspired words backed with love, not volume, that you will have "all ears" open and receiving.

There are two principles at work here: attention and obedience. Pastors, it starts with you. If God has your undivided attention and complete obedience, you can expect the same from your sheep. Yielded lives will bring about the renewal of this last great thrust of the church. Men's souls are dying and the church is their only hope. How will they hear unless a pastor is sent? It is time to go out into the fields because they are white unto harvest. It is time to get busy America. The world is waiting for the gospel you have to be brought over. It is time to look up for our redemption is drawing near. Even so come quickly, Lord Jesus.

Reference Notes

Chapter 5

1. Federer, *America's God and Country encycolpediaOf Quotations,* pp.370-317

Chapter 8

1. William L.Shirer, *The Rise and Fall of the Third Reich* (New York, NY: Simon and Schuster, 1960), pp. 248-249

Chapter 10

1. Billy Graham, "Atlanta: The Gospel for an Olympic City," *Decision,* Vol. 36, No. 1 (January 1995), p. 10

CPSIA information can be obtained at www.ICGtesting.com
Printed in the USA
LVOW07s1947190615

443189LV00001B/8/P